Bugs, Butterflies, Birds & Blooms™

Edited by Vicki Blizzard

the Needlecraft Shop

Bugs, Butterflies, Birds & Blooms

Copyright © 2004 The Needlecraft Shop,
Berne, Indiana 46711

EDITOR	Vicki Blizzard
ART DIRECTOR	Brad Snow
PUBLISHING SERVICES MANAGER	Brenda Gallmeyer
ASSOCIATE EDITOR	Tanya Turner
ASSISTANT ART DIRECTOR	Karen Allen
COPY SUPERVISOR	Michelle Beck
COPY EDITORS	Conor Allen
	Nicki Lehman
TECHNICAL EDITOR	June Sprunger
GRAPHIC PRODUCTION SUPERVISOR	Ronda Bechinski
COVER DESIGN	Edith Teegarden
GRAPHIC ARTIST	Debby Keel
PRODUCTION ASSISTANTS	Cheryl Kempf
	Marj Morgan
PHOTOGRAPHY	Tammy Christian
	Christena Green
	Kelly Heydinger
PHOTO STYLIST	Tammy Nussbaum
CHIEF EXECUTIVE OFFICER	John Robinson
PUBLISHING DIRECTOR	David McKee
EDITORIAL DIRECTOR	Vivian Rothe
BOOK MARKETING MANAGER	Craig Scott

Printed in the United States of America
First Printing: 2004
Library of Congress Number: 2004105955
ISBN: 1-57367-169-X

Welcome!

These are some of my favorite things: butterfly days and firefly nights—all sweetly scented with the heady fragrance of roses and other aromatic blossoms, the chirping of birds as they welcome the rising sun of spring

mornings, stately praying mantises sitting on drying cornstalks in my garden and flighty ladybugs landing on the pages of my book as I read in the sun.

I want to share some of my favorite things with you in the pages of this book. Our bugs aren't scary ones—they'll be right at home in your home. Our birds won't fly south in the winter and our blooms won't wilt and fade. You'll be pleased to know that most of these projects are quick as well as easy.

Celebrate life on a different plane as you stitch these cheery designs that will bring a smile to your face as you complete them. The smiles will continue as others see your finished projects!

Warm regards,

Vicki Blizzard

Spring

Summer

Autumn

Winter

CONTENTS · BUGS, BUTTERFLIES, BIRDS & BLOOMS **5**

Spring

Ah, spring—the glorious time, when buds awaken and the skies are filled with butterflies and bees! To help you celebrate, we offer a fun-filled assortment of projects, guaranteed to cheer and delight you throughout the season!

Dancing Daffodils Tissue Topper

Dimensional daffodils float on the breeze for an irresistible topper!

DESIGN BY KATHY WIRTH

Instructions

1. Cut plastic canvas according to graphs (this page and page 15).

2. Stitch top and sides following graphs, working uncoded areas with lime Continental Stitches. Do not work black Cross Stitches and French Knots at this time.

3. Overcast opening on top with lime; Overcast bottom edges of sides with paddy green.

4. Stitch flowers with white and yellow Continental Stitches, then orange French Knots, wrapping yarn around needle two times. Do not work black Cross Stitches and French Knots at this time. Overcast with white.

5. Attach large flowers to top and sides with four black French Knots where indicated, wrapping yarn around needle one time; attach small flowers with a Cross Stitch where indicated.

6. Using lime throughout, Whipstitch sides together, then Whipstitch sides to top. ●

GRAPHS CONTINUED ON PAGE 15

Skill Level

Beginner

Size

Fits boutique-style tissue box

Materials

- 2 sheets 7-count plastic canvas
- Coats & Clark Red Heart Classic worsted weight yarn Art. E267 as listed in color key
- Coats & Clark Red Heart Kids worsted weight yarn Art. E711 as listed in color key
- #16 tapestry needle

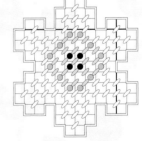

Dancing Daffodils Large Flower
12 holes x 13 holes
Cut 10

COLOR KEY	
Worsted Weight Yarn	**Yards**
☐ White #1	56
■ Black #12	5
☐ Yellow #230	7
■ Paddy green #686	13
☐ Lime #2652	67
Uncoded areas are lime #2652 Continental Stitches	
● Black #12 French Knot	
● Orange #2252 French Knot	13

Color numbers given are for Coats & Clark Red Heart Classic worsted weight yarn Art. E267 and Kids worsted weight yarn Art. E711.

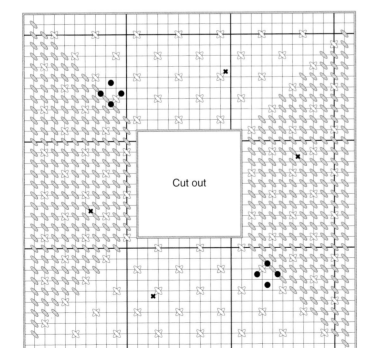

Dancing Daffodils Top
32 holes x 32 holes
Cut 1

Cut out

Spring Posy Pin

Show off your springtime spirit with this elegant ribbon rose!

DESIGN BY MARY T. COSGROVE

Skill Level

Intermediate

Size

1⅞ inches W x 2⅛ inches H

Materials

- Small amount 10-count plastic canvas
- Kreinik ⅛-inch Ribbon as listed in color key
- DMC 6-strand embroidery floss as listed in color key
- 7mm Bucilla ribbon from Plaid Enterprises Inc. as listed in color key
- 4mm Bucilla ribbon from Plaid Enterprises Inc. as listed in color key
- #18 tapestry needle
- 14-count metallic gold perforated paper by Yarn Tree
- 1-inch gold pin back
- Fabric glue

Instructions

1. Cut pin front and back from plastic canvas according to graph. Pin back will remain unstitched.

2. Stitch uncoded background on front with pearl ribbon Continental Stitches.

3. To make Spider Web rose, work five Straight Stitches for spokes with light mauve floss. Using hot pink silk ribbon, make rose petals by coming up in center hole, then work clockwise around spokes, weaving under and over spokes until they are covered.; bring ribbon through to back of canvas and secure.

4. Work hot pink French Knots for rose buds, wrapping needle three times. Work fern green Lazy Daisy Stitches for leaves around bottom petals of Spider Web rose and between rose buds. **Note:** *Three of the four Lazy Daisy Stitches are open at one end.*

5. Whipstitch unworked back to stitched front with vintage gold ribbon, keeping ribbon smooth and flat while stitching.

6. Using pin as a template, cut gold perforated paper to fit; glue to back of pin. Glue pin back to center back of gold perforated paper. ●

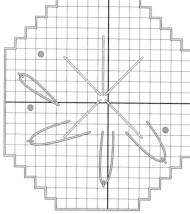

Spring Posy Pin Front & Back
18 holes x 20 holes
Cut 2, stitch 1

COLOR KEY	
⅛-Inch Ribbon	**Yards**
Uncoded background is pearl #032 Continental Stitches	3
✎ Vintage gold #002V Whipstitching	2
6-Strand Embroidery Floss	
✎ Light mauve #3689 Straight Stitch	1
7mm Silk Ribbon	
✎ Fern green #7020 Lazy Daisy Stitch	1
4mm Silk Ribbon	
● Hot pink #552 French Knot	1
Color numbers given are for Kreinik ⅛-inch Ribbon, DMC 6-strand embroidery floss and Bucilla 7mm and 4mm silk ribbon from Plaid Enterprises Inc.	

Bee Happy

These buzzy bugs are happy as can "bee" to cheer up any room!

DESIGN BY JANNA BRITTON

Instructions

1. Cut bees, frame and background from regular plastic canvas according to graphs (pages 10 and 11); cut bees' wings from plastic canvas heart (page 11), cutting away gray areas. Bees' wings will remain unstitched.

2. Stitch background following graph, working uncoded areas with blue jewel Continental Stitches. When background stitching is completed, work pale yellow floss Backstitches first, then work black pearl cotton embroidery. Do not Overcast.

3. Stitch and Overcast bees and frame, keeping curling ribbon smooth and flat while stitching. Embroider eyes and mouth on each bee when Background stitching is completed.

4. Using photo as a guide through step 5, shape each wing by overlapping ends; securely stitch one pair of wings to back of each bee.

5. Center frame over background; glue in place. Using black pearl cotton, tack bees to frame.

6. Hang as desired. ●

Skill Level
Beginner

Size
12¼ inches W x 7⅜ inches H, including bees' wings

Materials
- 2 sheets 7-count plastic canvas
- 6-inch Uniek QuickShape plastic canvas heart
- Uniek Needloft plastic canvas yarn as listed in color key
- Coats & Clark Red Heart Classic worsted weight yarn Art. E267 as listed in color key
- 3/16-inch-wide curling ribbon as listed in color key
- DMC 6-strand embroidery floss as listed in color key
- #3 pearl cotton as listed in color key
- #16 tapestry needle
- Low-temperature glue gun

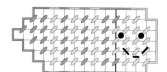

Bee Happy Bee
14 holes x 6 holes
Cut 2, reverse 1

COLOR KEY

	Plastic Canvas Yarn	Yards
■	Black #00	2
□	Lemon #20	6
■	Moss #25	9
■	Baby blue #36	7
□	White #41	8
■	Yellow #57	2

	Worsted Weight Yarn	
□	Lily pink #719	7
	Uncoded areas are blue jewel	
	#818 Continental Stitches	15

	3/16-Inch Curling Ribbon	
■	White	15

	6-Strand Embroidery Floss	
✎	Pale yellow #744 Backstitch	12

	#3 Pearl Cotton	
✎	Black Backstitch	
	and Straight Stitch	10
●	Black French Knot	

Color numbers given are for Uniek Needloft plastic canvas yarn, Coats & Clark Red Heart Classic worsted weight yarn Art. E267 and DMC 6-strand embroidery floss.

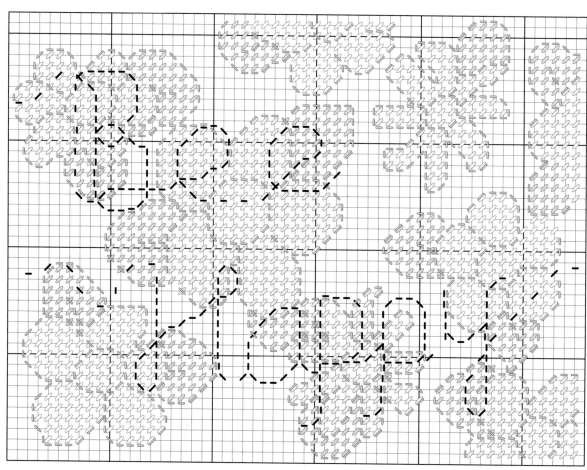

Bee Happy Background
56 holes x 42 holes
Cut 1

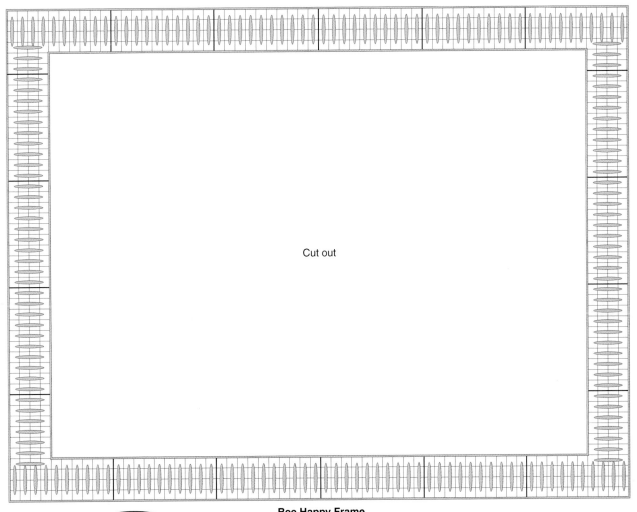

Cut out

Bee Happy Frame
60 holes x 46 holes
Cut 1

Bee's Wings
Cut 2 pairs as graphed,
cutting away gray areas
Do not stitch

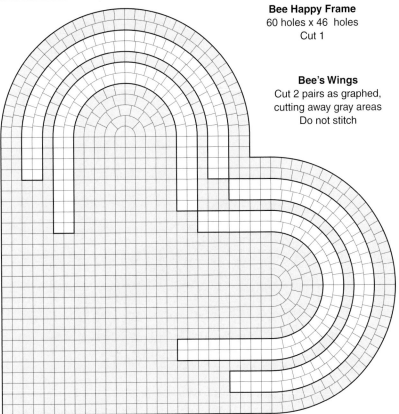

Purple Rose Vanity Tray

Pretty and powdery soft, this rosy tray will brighten your morning!

DESIGN BY ANGIE ARICKX

Skill Level

Beginner

Size

13½ inches W x ⅝ inches H x 10½ inches D

Materials

- 1¼ sheets 7-count plastic canvas
- Uniek Needloft plastic canvas yarn as listed in color key
- #16 tapestry needle

Instructions

1. Cut plastic canvas according to graphs.

2. Stitch pieces following graphs, working left half of base first; turn graph 180 degrees and work remaining half.

3. Using white, Overcast top edges of tray sides; Whipstitch sides to tray bottom, then Whipstitch sides together. ●

COLOR KEY	
Plastic Canvas Yarn	**Yards**
☐ Moss #25	6
■ Forest #29	4
☐ White #41	80
☐ Lilac #45	26
■ Purple #46	4
Uncoded areas are white #41 Continental Stitches	
Color numbers given are for Uniek Needloft plastic canvas yarn.	

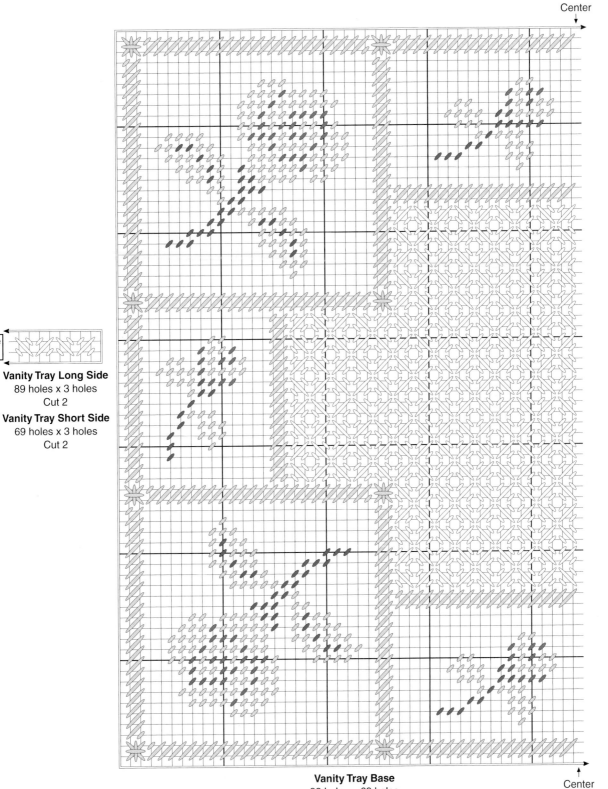

Continue pattern

Vanity Tray Long Side
89 holes x 3 holes
Cut 2

Vanity Tray Short Side
69 holes x 3 holes
Cut 2

Vanity Tray Base
89 holes x 69 holes
Cut 1
Stitch left half as graphed,
turn 180 degrees and
stitch remaining half

Center

Chubby Baby Birdies

Three birds of a feather perch together in this perky decoration!

DESIGN BY LEE LINDEMAN

Skill Level

Intermediate

Size

Birds: Approximately 3¾ inches W x 4¼ inches H x 3⅜ inches D
Large Leaf: 1½ inches W x 2⅝ inches H
Medium Leaf: 1¼ inches W x 2 inches H
Small Leaf: 1¼ inches W x 1⅞ inches H

Materials

- 2 sheets 7-count plastic canvas
- Uniek Needloft plastic canvas yarn as listed in color key
- #16 tapestry needle
- Polyester fiberfill
- 6 (8mm) brown animal eyes
- Small amount yellow craft foam
- 3 round toothpicks
- Pink blush
- Black fine-tip marker (optional)
- Ladybug button
- Multilimb branch
- Hot-glue gun

Cutting & Stitching

1. Cut plastic canvas according to graphs, cutting six body sections, two head pieces, two wings, two tails, one body top and one base for each bird.

2. From yellow craft foam, cut three triangles from ½- to ¾-inch-wide x ⅜- to ⅝-inch-long for top beak. Cut each bottom beak slightly smaller than matching top beak.

3. Following graphs, stitch and Overcast leaves, body tops, bases and wings, reversing one wing for each bird before stitching. Stitch body sections, heads and tails.

4. For each bird, Whipstitch six body sections together along side edges, easing as needed to fit. Overcast top and bottom edges of body.

5. Whipstitch two tail pieces together for each bird. Overcast bottom edges of each head from dot to dot. For each bird, Whipstitch two head pieces together around remaining edges.

Finishing

1. Stuff heads and bodies with fiberfill, then center and glue one body top and one base over body openings.

2. Using photo as a guide through step 6, add a little blush to chests of birds.

3. For head stability on each bird, cut one toothpick in half. Glue the two cut ends into neck opening, then glue pointed ends down into body top along front edge.

4. Glue on eyes and beaks. If desired, use fine-tip marker to add two dots to top of each beak near head for nostrils.

5. Glue wings to bodies on each side of chest; glue tails to body backs near bottom edge.

6. Glue birds and leaves to branch. Glue ladybug to one leaf. ●

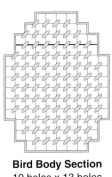

Bird Body Section
10 holes x 13 holes
Cut 18

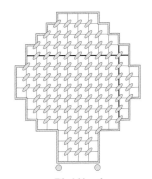

Bird Head
12 holes x 14 holes
Cut 6

Bird Base
13 holes x 12 holes
Cut 3

Bird Wing
10 holes x 5 holes
Cut 6, reverse 3

Bird Body Top
10 holes x 9 holes
Cut 3

Small Leaf
7 holes x 12 holes
Cut 5

Medium Leaf
7 holes x 13 holes
Cut 6

Large Leaf
9 holes x 17 holes
Cut 3

Bird Tail
12 holes x 15 holes
Cut 6

COLOR KEY	
Plastic Canvas Yarn	**Yards**
▨ Fern #23	20
☐ Bright blue #60	55
Color numbers given are for Uniek Needloft plastic canvas yarn.	

DANCING DAFFODILS TISSUE TOPPER CONTINUED FROM PAGE 7

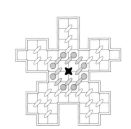

Dancing Daffodils Small Flower
10 holes x 10 holes
Cut 16

COLOR KEY	
Worsted Weight Yarn	**Yards**
☐ White #1	56
■ Black #12	5
☐ Yellow #230	7
▨ Paddy green #686	13
☐ Lime #2652	67
Uncoded areas are lime #2652 Continental Stitches	
● Black #12 French Knot	
● Orange #2252 French Knot	13
Color numbers given are for Coats & Clark Red Heart Classic worsted weight yarn Art. E267 and Kids worsted weight yarn Art. E711.	

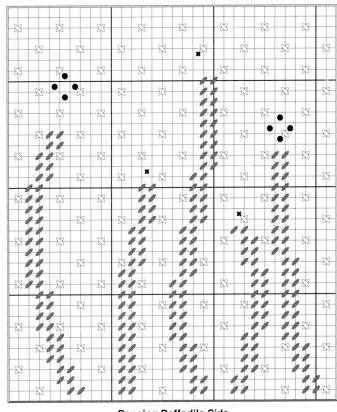

Dancing Daffodils Side
32 holes x 37 holes
Cut 4

Pot of Daffodils

Bring the garden indoors with this breezy bouquet of flowers!

DESIGN BY LEE LINDEMAN

Project Note

Keep stitching on backs of leaves, petals and trumpet pieces as neat as possible because they will be visible.

Instructions

1. Cut plastic canvas according to graphs, cutting five trumpet sections, five petals and one base for each flower, and four long leaves and four top and bottom pieces each for bent leaves.

2. From yellow plastic foam, cut five ⅛-inch-wide x 1⅞-inch-high stamens. Carefully make two 1¼-inch long cuts in one end of each stamen.

3. Cut plastic foam cone to fit in terra-cotta pot so that it fits about ¾ inch below top of rim; glue in place.

4. Paint dowels and beads with green paint; allow to dry.

5. Stitch and Overcast flower petals, flower base and long leaves following graphs.

6. Stitch trumpet sections and bent leaf pieces. With wrong sides facing, Whipstitch trumpet sections of each flower together along side edges, easing as needed to fit and Overcasting bottom edges while stitching; Overcast top edges with 1 ply tangerine.

7. For each bent leaf, Whipstitch one top and one bottom together; Overcast remaining edges.

Finishing

1. Using photo as a guide throughout finishing, glue right side of petals for each flower around bottom of trumpet, overlapping to fit.

2. Glue wrong side of each flower base to petals at bottom of flower.

3. For flower stems, glue one end of each dowel into a bead, then glue one side of bead to middle of flower base.

4. Poke stems in plastic foam and glue to secure. For each leaf, poke a long depression in plastic foam to hold end of leaf; glue leaf in depression.

5. Glue river rocks around stems and leaves, covering plastic foam.

6. Glue uncut end of one stamen in center of each trumpet. If desired, glue ladybug button to one leaf. ●

Skill Level

Intermediate

Size

Bouquet (in pot): Approximately 15¼ inches H

Materials

- 2 sheets 7-count plastic canvas
- Uniek Needloft plastic canvas yarn as listed in color key
- #16 tapestry needle
- 5 (12mm) wooden beads
- 5 (⅛-inch) dowels in various lengths
- Acrylic craft paint to match fern yarn
- Paintbrush
- Small amount yellow craft foam
- 4½-inch-high terra-cotta pot
- 9-inch x 3⅞-inch plastic foam cone
- Approximately 30 small smooth river rocks
- Ladybug button (optional)
- Hot-glue gun

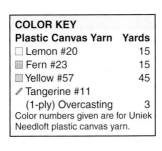

COLOR KEY	
Plastic Canvas Yarn	**Yards**
☐ Lemon #20	15
▨ Fern #23	15
☐ Yellow #57	45
✐ Tangerine #11 (1-ply) Overcasting	3
Color numbers given are for Uniek Needloft plastic canvas.	

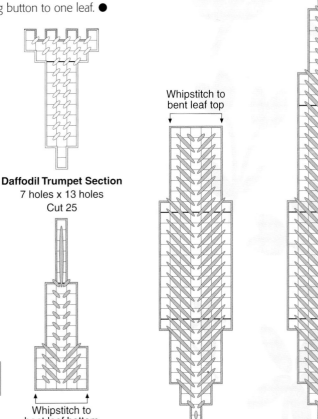

Daffodil Trumpet Section
7 holes x 13 holes
Cut 25

Whipstitch to bent leaf top

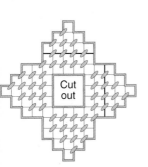

Daffodil Base
13 holes x 13 holes
Cut 5

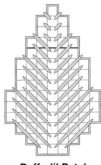

Daffodil Petal
9 holes x 14 holes
Cut 25

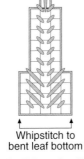

Whipstitch to bent leaf bottom

Daffodil Bent Leaf Top
5 holes x 16 holes
Cut 4

Daffodil Bent Leaf Bottom
7 holes x 28 holes
Cut 4

Daffodil Long Leaf
7 holes x 45 holes
Cut 4

Springtime Violets Coaster Set

The radiant blooms of these glorious coasters make any coffee break a gracious affair!

DESIGNS BY KRISTINE LOFFREDO

Skill Level

Beginner

Size

Coasters: 3⁷⁄₈ inches W x 3⁷⁄₈ inches H
Holder: 4¼ inches W x 4¼ inches H x 1⅛ inches D

Materials

- 1 sheet stiff 7-count plastic canvas
- Uniek Needloft plastic canvas yarn as listed in color key
- Kreinik Medium (#16) Braid as listed in color key
- #16 tapestry needle

Instructions

1. Cut plastic canvas according to graphs.
2. Stitch and Overcast coasters, working uncoded background with flesh tone Continental Stitches. Work black and vintage amber Backstitches and forest Straight Stitches when background stitching and Overcasting are completed.
3. Stitch holder pieces following graphs, leaving area indicated on base unstitched. Do not work vintage amber Backstitches at this time.
4. Using flesh tone through step 6, Whipstitch bottom edges of sides A to edges indicated on base, then Whipstitch sides A together along adjacent edges.
5. Whipstitch sides B to sides A where indicated, then Whipstitch adjacent edges of sides B together; Whipstitch sides B to base.
6. Whipstitch top to sides A and B; Overcast all remaining edges.
7. Work vintage amber Backstitches on top and sides B. Place coasters in holder. ●

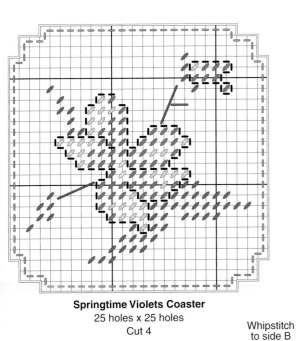

Springtime Violets Coaster
25 holes x 25 holes
Cut 4

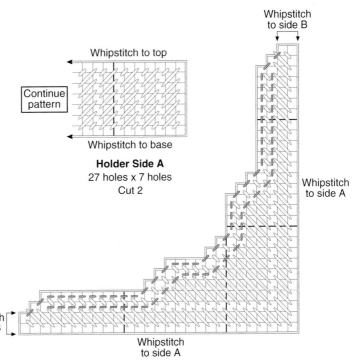

Whipstitch to top

Continue pattern

Whipstitch to base

Holder Side A
27 holes x 7 holes
Cut 2

Whipstitch to side B

Whipstitch to side A

Whipstitch to side B

Whipstitch to side A

Holder Top
27 holes x 27 holes
Cut 1

Whipstitch to top

Whipstitch to side A

Whipstitch to base

Holder Side B
27 holes x 7 holes
Cut 2, reverse 1

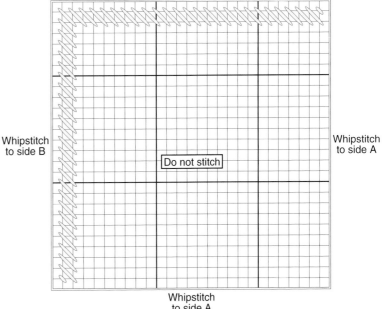

Whipstitch to side B

Whipstitch to side B

Whipstitch to side A

Do not stitch

Whipstitch to side A

Holder Base
27 holes x 27 holes
Cut 1

COLOR KEY	
Plastic Canvas Yarn	**Yards**
☐ Lemon #20	1
■ Forest #29	5
☐ Lilac #45	3
■ Purple #46	4
☐ Flesh tone #56	50
Uncoded background on coasters is flesh tone #56 Continental Stitches	
✦ Forest #29 Straight Stitch	
Medium (#16) Braid	6
✦ Black #005C Backstitch	7
✦ Vintage amber #150V Backstitch	
Color numbers given are for Uniek Needloft plastic canvas yarn and Kreinik Medium (#16) Braid.	

Tulip Picnic Pockets

Keep picnic ware and napkins tidy in pretty floral pockets!

DESIGN BY ALIDA MACOR

Skill Level
Beginner

Size
4½ inches W x 8⅞ inches H

Materials
Each Pocket
- ⅔ sheet white 7-count plastic canvas
- Uniek Needloft plastic canvas yarn as listed in color key
- #16 tapestry needle

Project Note
Instructions and amounts given are for one pocket.
Use color of choice for flower part of tulips. Flower colors used on samples were tangerine, yellow, watermelon and purple.

Instructions
1. Cut plastic canvas according to graphs. Pocket back will remain unstitched.

2. Stitch front following graph, leaving areas indicated unstitched.

3. Place pocket front on pocket back, then Whipstitch together, Overcasting around top and side edges of back while Whipstitching. Stitch in every hole along bottom edges and along diagonal edges at top; stitch in every other hole along sides and top edge, concealing yarn ends neatly. Top edges of pocket front will remain unstitched. ●

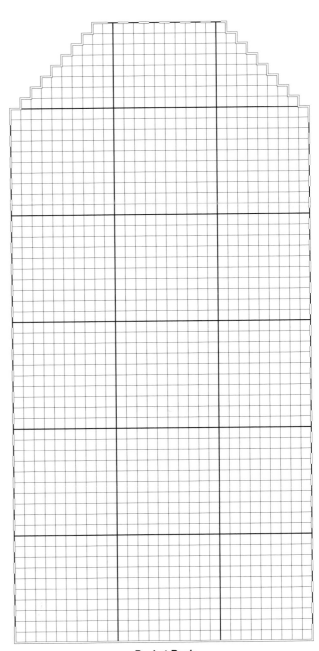

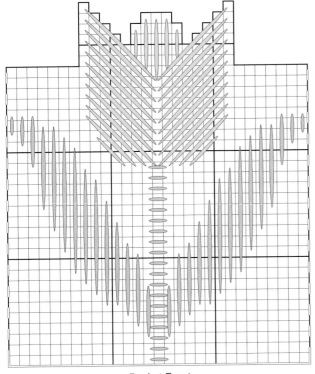

Pocket Front
29 holes x 34 holes
Cut 1

Pocket Back
29 holes x 58 holes
Cut 1
Do not stitch

Spring Calendar

Breeze into spring with the freshness and charm of this lovely floral calendar frame!

DESIGN BY ANGIE ARICKX

Skill Level
Beginner

Size
13½ inches W x 11 inches H;
fits calendar sheet 11 inches W x
8½ inches H

Materials
- 3 sheets 7-count plastic canvas
- Uniek Needloft plastic canvas yarn as listed in color key
- #16 tapestry needle
- Sawtooth hanger
- Hot-glue gun

Project Note
Some graphs are shared with similar calendars in other chapters of this book. Colors used for each season are given with the graphs and/or the instructions for that season.

Instructions
1. Cut plastic canvas according to graphs (this page and pages 24 and 25). Cut one 81-hole x 65-hole piece for calendar frame back.
2. Stitch and Overcast bunnies, fence, violets and leaves following graphs, working uncoded areas on bunnies with camel Continental Stitches. Work Backstitches and French Knots on bunnies when background stitching is completed.
3. Stitch calendar frame front, leaving area shaded with yellow unworked for now. Overcast inside and outside edges. Center spacer, then frame back over unworked area on wrong side of calendar front.
Note: Spacer should be between frame front and back. Complete pattern stitch on frame front in shaded yellow area, working through all three layers.
4. Using photo as a guide, glue fence, bunnies, violets and leaves to frame front. Glue hanger to frame back. Insert calendar through opening on right side. ●

COLOR KEY

Plastic Canvas Yarn	Yards
☐ Pink #07	1
☐ Fern #23	8
■ Royal #32	2
☐ White #41	13
■ Watermelon #55	1
☐ Bright blue #60	40
■ Bright purple #64	12
Uncoded areas on bunnies are camel #43 Continental Stitches	5
⁄ Camel #43 Overcasting	
⁄ Black #00 Straight Stitch	1
● Watermelon #55 French Knot	
Color numbers given are for Uniek Needloft plastic canvas yarn.	

Calendar Leaf
4 holes x 4 holes
Cut 22 for spring; stitch as graphed
Cut 14 for summer; stitch with holly

Spring Calendar Violet
7 holes x 7 holes
Cut 12

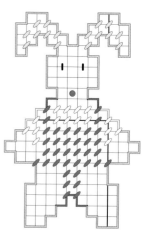

Spring Calendar Bunny
13 holes x 20 holes
Cut 2

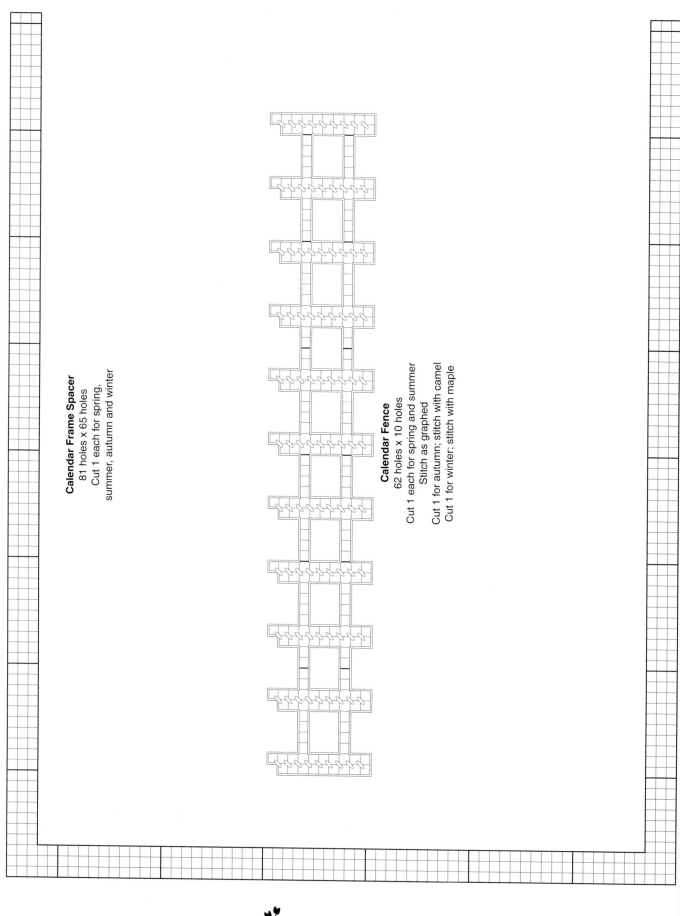

Calendar Frame Spacer
81 holes x 65 holes
Cut 1 each for spring,
summer, autumn and winter

Calendar Fence
62 holes x 10 holes
Cut 1 each for spring and summer
Stitch as graphed
Cut 1 for autumn; stitch with camel
Cut 1 for winter; stitch with maple

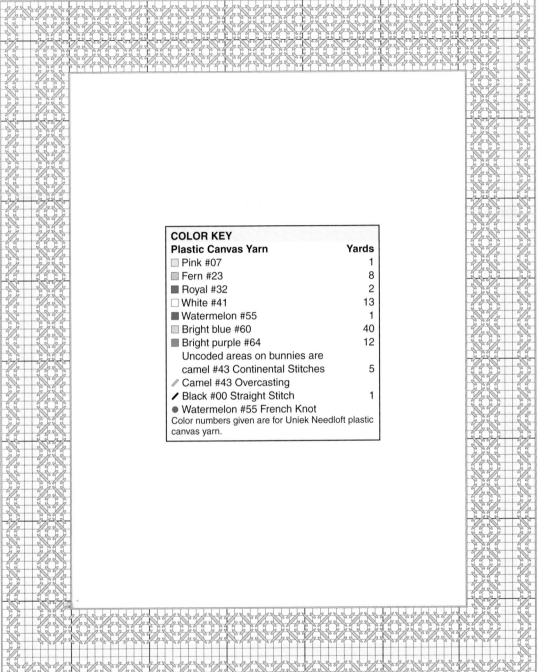

COLOR KEY

Plastic Canvas Yarn	Yards
☐ Pink #07	1
☐ Fern #23	8
■ Royal #32	2
☐ White #41	13
■ Watermelon #55	1
☐ Bright blue #60	40
■ Bright purple #64	12
Uncoded areas on bunnies are camel #43 Continental Stitches	5
⁄ Camel #43 Overcasting	
╱ Black #00 Straight Stitch	1
● Watermelon #55 French Knot	

Color numbers given are for Uniek Needloft plastic canvas yarn.

Calendar Frame Front
85 holes x 69 holes

Cut 1 for spring; stitch as graphed
Cut 1 for summer; stitch with fern
Cut 1 for autumn; stitch with beige
Cut 1 for winter; stitch with holly

Friends in Flight

Entertain the younger set with the playful charm of these butterfly buddies!

DESIGNS BY RUBY THACKER

Skill Level
Intermediate

Size
Bunny Butterfly Wings: 3⅞ inches W x 3¾ inches H (vest and wings fit 5-inch bunny)
Teddy Bear Butterfly Wings: 4¾ inches W x 3⅞ inches H (vest, hood and wings fit 5-inch teddy bear)

Materials
Each
- Uniek Needloft plastic canvas yarn as listed in color key
- #16 tapestry needle

Bunny
- 1 sheet clear 7-count plastic canvas
- Uniek Needloft solid metallic craft cord as listed in color key
- 5-inch bunny

Teddy Bear
- ½ sheet clear stiff 7-count plastic canvas
- ¼ sheet black 7-count plastic canvas
- 6-strand embroidery floss as listed in color key
- 5-inch teddy bear
- 12 inches ⅛-inch-wide black satin ribbon
- 2 (³⁄₁₆-inch) black pompoms
- 3 inches black covered wire
- Clear craft glue

Bunny
1. Cut back wings, front wings and vest from clear regular plastic canvas according to graphs.
2. Stitch wings and vest following graphs, reversing one front wing, then working piece with reverse stitches.
3. Using sandstone, Overcast armhole openings and top and bottom edges of vest. Work solid gold Straight Stitches, forming a Cross Stitch across front of vest.
4. Using moss through step 5, with right

sides together, Whipstitch front wings between brackets to side edges of vest, Overcasting edges with red dots while Whipstitching.
5. Put vest on bunny; fold wings out. Whipstitch wrong sides of front and back wings together around remaining edges.

Teddy Bear
1. Following graphs throughout, cut back and front wings (page 28) from clear stiff plastic canvas; cut vest, hood center panel

and hood side panels (page 28) from black plastic canvas.

2. Stitch hood and vest pieces following graphs, reversing one side panel before stitching.

3. Stitch back wings following graph, working uncoded areas with black Continental Stitches. Stitch front wings, reversing one wing, then working piece with reverse stitches.

4. When background stitching on wings is completed, work white floss Backstitches and black yarn Straight Stitches.

5. Overcast armhole openings and top and bottom edges of vest following graph.

6. Using black through step 7, attach vest and wings to teddy bear following steps 4 and 5 for bunny.

7. For hood, Whipstitch holes A of side panels and center panel together, then Whipstitch holes B together; Overcast remaining edges.

8. Thread black ribbon behind stitches along entire bottom edge of assembled hood, making ribbon tails even. Fold black covered wire in half and thread ends from back to front through holes with blue dots on hood center panel. Glue pompoms to wire ends.

9. Place hood on bear and tie with a bow under chin. ●

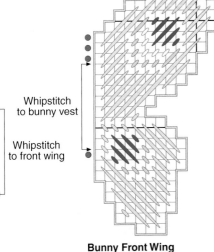

Bunny Front Wing
12 holes x 24 holes
Cut 2 from clear regular
Stitch 1 as graphed
Reverse 1 and work
with reverse stitches

Whipstitch to bunny vest

Whipstitch to front wing

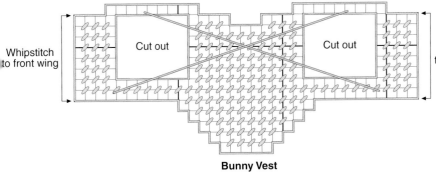

Whipstitch to front wing

Bunny Vest
33 holes x 14 holes
Cut 1 from clear regular

Cut out

Cut out

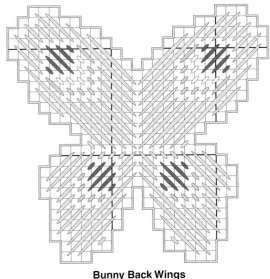

Bunny Back Wings
25 holes x 24 holes
Cut 1 from clear regular

COLOR KEY

Plastic Canvas Yarn	Yards
■ Black #00	22
▨ Sandstone #16	5
▨ Moss #25	12
▨ Christmas green #28	2
□ White #41 (bunny wings)	1
▨ Bittersweet #52	7
▨ Turquoise #54	3
Uncoded areas on teddy bear wings	
are black #00 Continental Stitches	
╱ Black #00 Straight Stitch	
Solid Metallic Craft Cord	
□ Solid gold #20	2
╱ Solid gold #20 Straight Stitch	
6-Strand Embroidery Floss	
╱ White Backstitch (teddy bear wings)	8

Color numbers given are for Uniek Needloft plastic canvas yarn and solid metallic craft cord.

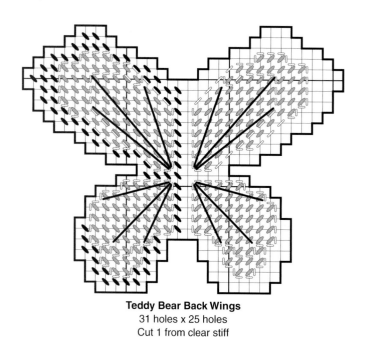

Teddy Bear Back Wings
31 holes x 25 holes
Cut 1 from clear stiff

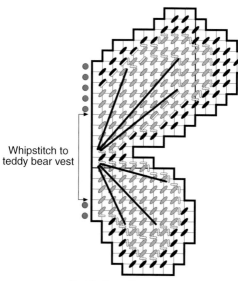

Whipstitch to
teddy bear vest

Teddy Bear Front Wing
15 holes x 25 holes
Cut 2 from clear stiff
Stitch 1 as graphed
Reverse 1 and work
with reverse stitches

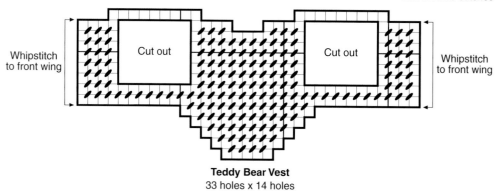

Whipstitch
to front wing

Cut out

Cut out

Whipstitch
to front wing

Teddy Bear Vest
33 holes x 14 holes
Cut 1 from black

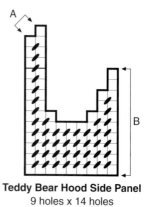

A

B

Teddy Bear Hood Side Panel
9 holes x 14 holes
Cut 2 from black, reverse 1

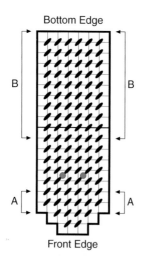

Bottom Edge

B

B

A

A

Front Edge

Teddy Bear Hood Center Panel
7 holes x 19 holes
Cut 1 from black

COLOR KEY	
Plastic Canvas Yarn	**Yards**
■ Black #00	22
▢ Sandstone #16	5
▢ Moss #25	12
▨ Christmas green #28	2
▢ White #41 (bunny wings)	1
▨ Bittersweet #52	7
▨ Turquoise #54	3
Uncoded areas on teddy bear wings are black #00 Continental Stitches	
╱ Black #00 Straight Stitch	
Solid Metallic Craft Cord	
▨ Solid gold #20	2
╱ Solid gold #20 Straight Stitch	
6-Strand Embroidery Floss	
╱ White Backstitch (teddy bear wings)	8
Color numbers given are for Uniek Needloft plastic canvas yarn and solid metallic craft cord.	

Blossoms & Bluebirds

Beautifully detailed and delicately trimmed, this terrific topper will sweeten the season!

DESIGN BY SUSAN LEINBERGER

Project Note

Use #16 tapestry needle with full strand yarn and #20 tapestry needle with 1-ply yarn and embroidery floss.

Cutting & Stitching

1. Cut plastic canvas according to graphs (page 30).

2. Stitch pieces following graphs, working uncoded areas with white Continental Stitches.

3. When background stitching is completed, use full strand of yarn to work all pink and bright blue Backstitches and camel Straight Stitches for birds' beaks on sides A only.

4. Use 1-ply yarn to work moss Backstitches, camel Straight Stitches for birds' beaks on top piece and lemon

French Knots for flower centers, wrapping needle one time.

5. Use 6-ply floss to work French Knot eyes for each bird on sides A and 2-ply floss to work French Knot eyes for birds on top piece, wrapping needle one time for all French Knots.

6. Using pink throughout, Overcast inside edges of top and bottom edges of sides. Whipstitch sides together, then Whipstitch sides to top.

7. Cut two 18-inch lengths ⁷⁄₈-inch-wide ribbon. Hold both lengths together and tie in a bow, adjusting loops and tails as desired. Cut a notch in ribbon tails.

8. Using photo as a guide, glue this bow to top; glue three 1⁵⁄₈-inch-long bows to center of each side B. ●

Skill Level

Beginner

Size

Fits boutique-style tissue box

Materials

- 2 sheets 7-count plastic canvas
- Uniek Needloft plastic canvas yarn as listed in color key
- 6-strand embroidery floss as listed in color key
- #16 tapestry needle
- #20 tapestry needle
- 1 yard ⁷⁄₈-inch-wide pink gingham ribbon
- 6 (1⁵⁄₈-inch-long) pink #117 Stylish Accents Ribbon Accessories bows by C.M. Offray & Son Inc.
- Hot-glue gun

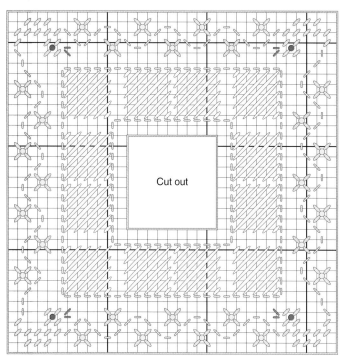

Blossoms & Bluebirds Top
33 holes x 33 holes
Cut 1

COLOR KEY

Plastic Canvas Yarn	Yards
☐ Pink #07	20
☐ Moss #25	10
■ Royal #32	10
☐ White #41	70
☐ Camel #43	3
☐ Bright blue #60	16
Uncoded areas are white #41 Continental Stitches	
✐ Pink #07 (2-ply) Backstitch	
✐ Moss #25 (1-ply) Backstitch	
✐ Camel #43 (2-ply) Straight Stitch	
✐ Camel #43 (1-ply) Straight Stitch	
✐ Bright blue #60 (2-ply) Backstitch	
○ Lemon #20 (1-ply) French Knot	5
6-Strand Embroidery Floss	
● Black (6-ply) French Knot	1
● Black (1-ply) French Knot	

Color numbers given are for Uniek Needloft plastic canvas yarn.

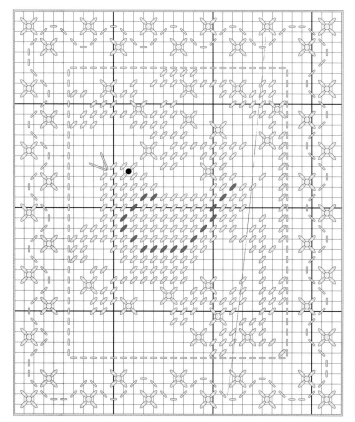

Blossoms & Bluebirds Side A
33 holes x 39 holes
Cut 2

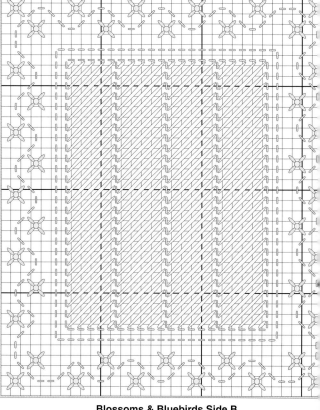

Blossoms & Bluebirds Side B
33 holes x 39 holes
Cut 2

Butterflies & Blooms Tic-Tac-Toe

This delightful centerpiece celebrates the youthful joy of spring!

DESIGNS BY RUBY THACKER

Project Note

Use #16 tapestry needle with worsted weight yarn and #18 tapestry needle with 6-strand embroidery floss.

Instructions

1. Cut game board from 7-count plastic canvas; cut butterflies and blooms from 10-count plastic canvas according to graphs (page 32).

2. Stitch and Overcast pieces following graphs, working butterflies and blooms with floss and game board with yarn.

3. When Background stitching is completed, work black Straight Stitch at center of each butterfly. ●

Skill Level

Beginner

Size

Game Board: 6 inches square
Butterflies: 1 5/8 inches W x 1 1/8 inches H
Blooms: 1 1/8 inches W x 1 1/8 inches H

Materials

- 1/2 sheet 7-count plastic canvas
- 1/4 sheet 10-count plastic canvas
- Coats & Clark Red Heart Super Saver worsted weight yarn Art. E300 as listed in color key
- DMC 6-strand embroidery floss as listed in color key
- #16 tapestry needle
- #18 tapestry needle

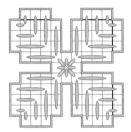

Bloom Game Piece
11 holes x 11 holes
Cut 5 from 10-count

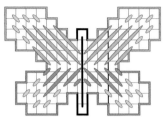

Butterfly Game Piece
15 holes x 10 holes
Cut 5 from 10-count

COLOR KEY	
Worsted Weight Yarn	**Yards**
☐ White #311	16
☐ Light sage #631	4
6-Strand Embroidery Floss	
☐ Pumpkin #971	4
☐ Bright canary #973	3
☐ Medium electric blue #996	3
☐ Light cyclamen pink #3806	6
✐ Black #310 Straight Stitch	
and Overcasting	2

Color numbers given are for Coats & Clark Red Heart Super Saver worsted weight yarn Art. E300 and DMC 6-strand embroidery floss.

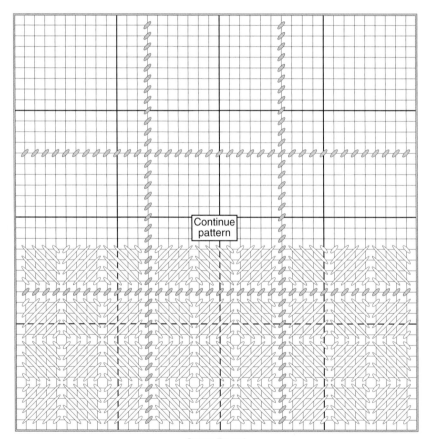

Continue pattern

Game Board
39 holes x 39 holes
Cut 1 from 7-count

Spring Bug Welcome

This cute little critter will make your guests feel as snug as a bug in a … nest!

DESIGN BY JANELLE GIESE

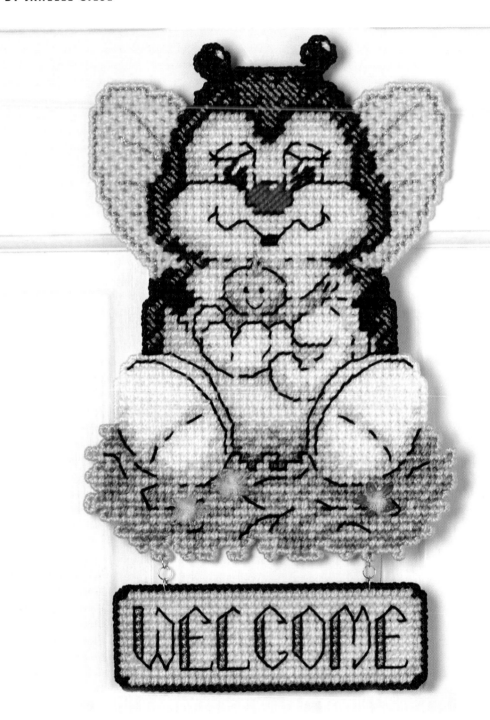

Skill Level
Advanced

Size
7½ inches W x 12½ inches H

Materials
- 1 sheet stiff 7-count plastic canvas
- Uniek Needloft plastic canvas yarn as listed in color key
- Kreinik Heavy (#32) Braid as listed in color key
- #5 pearl cotton as listed in color key
- #3 pearl cotton as listed in color key
- #16 tapestry needle
- Sawtooth hanger
- 6 (7mm) nickel jump rings
- Needle-nose pliers

Project Note
The triangle, heart, square, inverted triangle and diamond shapes designate Continental Stitches.

The sign graph is shared with the other bug welcome designs in other chapters of this book. Colors used for each season are given with the graphs and/or the instructions for that season.

Instructions
1. Cut plastic canvas according to graphs.
2. Stitch and Overcast welcome sign following graph, working uncoded background with eggshell Continental Stitches.
3. When background stitching on sign is completed, work pink heavy braid Straight Stitches over lavender Continental Stitches. Using black #3 pearl cotton, embroider remaining portions of lettering.
4. Stitch and Overcast bug, working uncoded areas with baby yellow Continental Stitches.
5. When background stitching is completed, use black #5 pearl cotton to work Straight Stitches over lavender Continental Stitches. Backstitch pink heavy braid accents on wings.
6. Using a full strand yarn, Straight Stitch eye and antennae highlights with white, tuft atop bird's head with sail blue, and beak with diagonal beige stitches and one vertical baby yellow stitch. Use black #3 pearl cotton to embroider features, wrapping French Knots one time for bird's eyes.
7. Use 1-ply yarn to embroider Lazy Daisy Stitch flowers with red, pumpkin and sail blue.
8. To form flower centers, draw a full strand baby yellow yarn through flower center from front to back, leaving yarn tail in front. Work a couple of Backstitches in stitching on back side, then bring yarn through flower center to front; trim yarn ends and fluff with fingers.
9. Sew sawtooth hanger to top center back of bug's head with #5 pearl cotton. Using needle-nose pliers, join bug to sign by forming two chains of three jump rings each, attaching top and bottom jump rings through holes indicated with red dots. ●

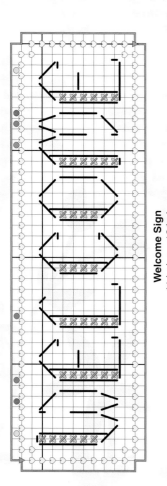

Welcome Sign
41 holes x 13 holes
Cut 1 for each season
Stitch as graphed for spring
For summer, replace lavender yarn with red yarn and pink braid with red braid
For autumn, replace lavender yarn with rust yarn and pink braid with orange braid
For winter, replace lavender yarn with lilac yarn and pink braid with lilac braid

COLOR KEY	
Plastic Canvas Yarn	**Yards**
▽ Black #00	8
◢ Red #01	1
◢ Lavender #05	3
◢ Cinnamon #14	1
◇ Moss #25	1
■ Sail blue #35	2
♡ Baby blue #36	1
△ Silver #37	4
◢ Eggshell #39	13
♡ Beige #40	11
☐ White #41	9
△ Camel #43	5
Uncoded background on bug is baby yellow #21 Continental Stitches	7
Uncoded background on welcome sign is eggshell #39 Continental Stitches	
╱ Baby yellow #21 Straight Stitch	
╱ Sail blue #35 Straight Stitch	
╱ Beige #40 Straight Stitch	
╱ White #41 Straight Stitch	
◗ Red #01 Lazy Daisy Stitch	
◗ Pumpkin #12 Lazy Daisy Stitch	1
◗ Sail blue #35 Lazy Daisy Stitch	
Heavy (#32) Braid	
╱ Pink #007 Backstitch and Straight Stitch	4
#3 Pearl Cotton	
╱ Black Backstitch and Straight Stitch	1
● Black French Knot	
#5 Pearl Cotton	
╱ Black Straight Stitch	7
Color numbers given are for Uniek Needloft plastic canvas yarn and Kreinik Heavy (#32) Braid.	

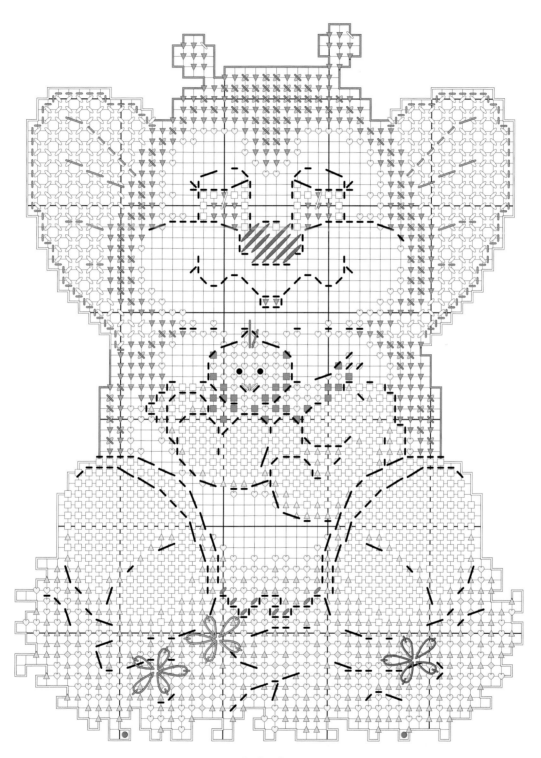

Spring Bug
49 holes x 67 holes
Cut 1

Robin on a Stick

This handsome harbinger of spring will feather your nest with love!

DESIGN BY KATHY WIRTH

Skill Level

Intermediate

Size

Approximately 9½ inches W x
20 inches H

Materials

- 1½ sheets 7-count plastic canvas
- Coats & Clark Red Heart Classic worsted weight yarn Art. E267 as listed in color key
- #3 pearl cotton as listed in color key
- #16 tapestry needle
- #18 tapestry needle
- Small amount fiberfill
- 12 inches black 24-gauge wire
- 1-inch Favorite Findings red Valentine's Heart button #80 from Blumenthal Lansing Co.
- 12 inches ³/₁₆-inch hardwood dowel
- 5-inch-high x 2¼-inch-diameter Create A Tassel large clown head #84927 wooden tassel top from Toner Plastics
- Acrylic craft paints: light blue, black, white, yellow, coral and red (to match yarn colors)
- Paintbrushes
- Finishing spray
- Sandpaper
- Pencil
- Hot-glue gun

Project Note

Use #16 tapestry needle with yarn and #18 tapestry needle with pearl cotton.

Cutting & Stitching

1. Cut plastic canvas according to graphs (page 38).

2. Stitch one robin following graph; reverse remaining robin and stitch, working stitches in opposite direction.

3. Stitch two wings as graphed, reverse remaining two wings and work stitches in opposite direction.

4. When background stitching is completed, work black yarn French Knot for each eye and black pearl cotton Backstitches and Straight Stitches on each beak, tail and wing.

5. Matching edges, Whipstitch wing fronts to wing backs. Whipstitch robin pieces together, sandwiching fiberfill between and Overcasting bottom edges between blue dots.

6. Glue wings to body as in photo.

Painting

1. Lightly sand tassel top and dowel; wipe clean. Paint dowel yellow.

2. Paint tassel top as follows, allowing paint to dry between each step: head and base, coral; body, blue; band, white; black lines in band to form checks. To add red dots to coral sections, dip end of brush handle in red paint, then dab onto wood.

3. Spray all painted surfaces with protective finishing spray.

Final Assembly

1. Run one end of wire through holes in button and twist to secure. Run remaining end of wire through end of beak and secure. Curl wire around pencil.

2. Insert one end of dowel through hole in tassel top all the way to the bottom. Turn upside down and drip hot glue inside to secure dowel.

3. Place glue on remaining end of dowel and insert in opening at bottom of bird, leaving about 4 inches of dowel exposed. ●

COLOR KEY

Worsted Weight Yarn	Yards
☐ White #1	5
▦ Black #12	5
☐ Cornmeal #220	1
▨ Medium coral #252	9
☐ Blue jewel #818	16
▦ Light periwinkle #827	34
▨ Country red #914	3
● Black #12 French Knot	

#3 Pearl Cotton

✐ Black Backstitch and Straight Stitch	7

Color numbers given are for Coats & Clark Red Heart Classic worsted weight yarn Art. E267.

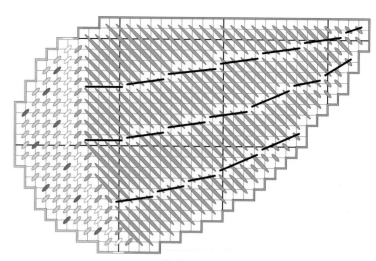

Robin Wing
34 holes x 22 holes
Cut 4
Stitch 2 as graphed
Reverse 2 and work stitches
in opposite direction

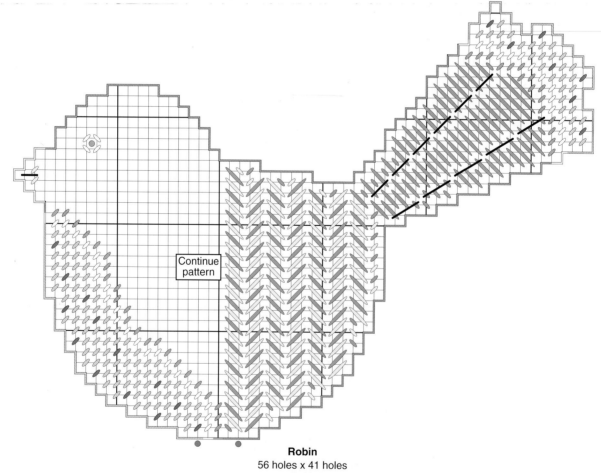

Continue pattern

Robin
56 holes x 41 holes
Cut 2
Stitch 1 as graphed
Reverse 1 and work stitches
in opposite direction

Pansy Coasters & Holder

Pick a peck of pansies to adorn your favorite table!

DESIGNS BY KATHY WIRTH

Project Note

Use #16 tapestry needle with yarn and #20 tapestry needle with pearl cotton.

Instructions

1. Cut plastic canvas according to graphs (page 40). Cut one 21-hole x 13-hole piece for holder bottom. Holder bottom will remain unstitched.

2. Trace around a coaster onto backing paper of self-adhesive felt, smoothing outline. Cut out slightly inside traced line, then dry-fit on coaster, trimming as needed; use as pattern to cut out three more felt pieces.

3. Stitch four coaster pieces and holder front, back and ends following graphs, working uncoded areas on holder pieces with yellow Continental Stitches. Four coaster pieces will remain unstitched to be used as liners.

4. Using black pearl cotton, work French Knots in center of each coaster and lettering on holder front only; work bright purple French Knots on holder front, back and ends.

5. For each coaster, place one unworked liner under one stitched coaster, then Whipstitch together with yellow and bright purple following graph. Apply felt to back of each coaster.

6. Using yellow throughout, Whipstitch side edges of front and back to ends from blue dot to blue dot, easing as necessary to fit, then Whipstitch unstitched bottom to front, back and ends. Overcast remaining edges. ●

Skill Level

Beginner

Size

Coasters: 4¾ inches W x 4½ inches H
Holder: 5½ inches W x 2⅝ inches H x 2⅛ inches D

Materials

- 2½ sheets 7-count plastic canvas
- Uniek Needloft plastic canvas yarn as listed in color key
- #3 pearl cotton as listed in color key
- #16 tapestry needle
- #20 tapestry needle
- 1 sheet black self-adhesive felt
- #18 tapestry needle

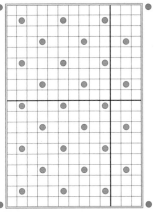

Pansy Coaster Holder End
13 holes x 19 holes
Cut 2

Pansy Coaster
31 holes x 29 holes
Cut 8, stitch 4

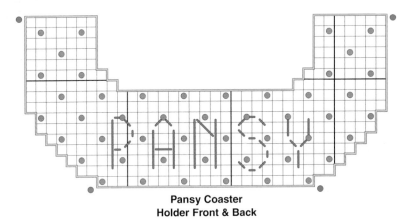

Pansy Coaster
Holder Front & Back
35 holes x 16 holes
Cut 2
Stitch letters on front only

COLOR KEY	
Plastic Canvas Yarn	**Yards**
■ Black #00	8
☐ Yellow #57	36
■ Bright purple #64	23
Uncoded backgrounds on holder pieces are yellow #57 Continental Stitches	
● Bright purple #64 French Knot	
#3 Pearl Cotton	
╱ Black Backstitch	1
● Black French Knot	
Color numbers given are for Uniek Needloft plastic canvas yarn.	

Mother's Nest

Make your nest the best in town with this fluffy
feathered friend!

DESIGN BY JANELLE GIESE

Skill Level

Advanced

Size

7½ inches W x 12½ inches H

Materials

- ⅔ sheet 7-count plastic canvas
- Coats & Clark Red Heart Classic worsted weight yarn Art. E267 as listed in color key
- Kreinik Medium (#16) Braid as listed in color key
- Kreinik Cord as listed in color key
- DMC #5 pearl cotton as listed in color key
- Small amount 6-strand embroidery floss to match pink yarn
- #16 tapestry needle
- 4 miniature silk flowers to coordinate with yarn colors
- Small amount of Spanish moss
- Sawtooth hanger
- Thick white glue

Project Note

The triangle, heart, square, inverted triangle and diamond shapes designate Continental Stitches.

Instructions

1. Cut plastic canvas according to graph.
2. Stitch and Overcast motif following graph, working uncoded background on top banner with lily pink Continental Stitches; work uncoded background on bird and bottom banner with blue jewel Continental Stitches. Fill in background on leaves with light sage Straight Stitches.
3. Using tan, eggshell and cornmeal, work Turkey Loop Stitches on breast of bird as indicated, making loops ⅝-inch high. Cut loops, then fluff by separating yarn strands with a needle. Trim fluffed ends slightly to shape.
4. Using full strands of yarn, Straight Stitch leaf stems with tan, feathers atop head with blue jewel and two small stitches for each eye with black. Using 2-ply eggshell, form a small stitch for each eye highlight where indicated.
5. Using antique gold medium braid and very dark garnet pearl cotton for laid threads and using antique gold

cord for couching thread, work the word "Mothers" on top banner. **Note:** *The pearl cotton is used as a shadow for the metallic lettering and changes position in relation to the antique gold braid.*
6. Work pearl cotton embroidery, wrapping French Knot in the letter "i" two times. Straight Stitch straw in nest with full strand tan. Straight Stitch antique gold braid accent lines against tan straw Straight Stitches and black pearl cotton letters.

7. Draw stem of a miniature silk flower under stitches of beak where indicated on graph; curl end.
8. Using yarn needle, draw small clusters of Spanish moss under stitches of beak with flower stem and under straw Straight Stitches on nest where indicated on graph. Glue flowers to nest where indicated.
9. Sew sawtooth hanger to center back at top of banner using matching floss. ●

COLOR KEY	
Worsted Weight Yarn	**Yards**
⬩ Black #12	1
♡ Eggshell #111	4
⬩ Cornmeal #220	3
☐ Tan #334	6
△ Warm brown #336	2
▼ Mid brown #339	2
⬩ Nickel #401	3
△ Silver #412	2
◇ Light sage #631	3
■ Dark sage #633	4
♥ Pale rose #755	2
⬩ Cameo rose #759	1
▼ Light periwinkle #827	4
Uncoded areas on top banner are lily pink #719 Continental Stitches	6
Uncoded areas on bird and bottom banner are blue jewel #8181 Continental Stitches	3
⬩ Lily pink #719 Overcasting	
⬩ Eggshell #111 Straight Stitch and Turkey Loop Stitch	
⬩ Cornmeal #220 Turkey Loop Stitch	
⬩ Tan #334 Straight Stitch and Turkey Loop Stitch	
⬩ Light sage #631 Straight Stitch	
⬩ Blue jewel #818 Straight Stitch	
#5 Pearl Cotton	
⬩ Black #310 Backstitch and Straight Stitch	7
⬩ Very dark garnet #902 Backstitch	2
● Black #310 French Knot	
Medium #16 Braid	
⬩ Antique gold #205C Straight Stitch and laid Couching Stitch	3
Cord	
⬩ Antique gold #205C Couching Stitch	3
╱ Spanish moss placement	
○ Attach flower	
Color numbers given are for Coats & Clark Red Heart Classic worsted weight yarn Art. E267, DMC #5 pearl cotton and Kreinik Cord and Medium (#16) Braid.	

Mother's Nest Motif
57 holes x 46 holes
Cut 1

Flower Basket Wall Hanging

A basketful of blooming beauty is just the thing to welcome spring!

DESIGN BY RONDA BRYCE

Skill Level
Beginner

Size
11 inches W x 13 inches H

Materials
- 2 sheets country blue Uniek QuickCount 7-count plastic canvas
- 1 sheet almond Uniek QuickCount 7-count plastic canvas
- 1 sheet forest green Uniek QuickCount 7-count plastic canvas
- 1 sheet clear Uniek QuickCount 7-count plastic canvas
- Uniek Needloft plastic canvas yarn as listed in color key
- #16 tapestry needle
- 5 (8mm) white pearl beads
- 3 (3/8-inch) white pearl buttons
- 1 butterfly and 4 flower In the Garden #272 Favorite Findings buttons from Blumenthal Lansing Co.
- 3 (3¼-inch) white pearl sprays
- Hand-sewing needle
- Sewing thread: white, yellow, pink, green, blue
- Sawtooth hanger

Instructions

1. Following graphs throughout, cut background from almond plastic canvas (page 46); frame pieces, handle and basket from country blue plastic canvas (page 47); and leaves from forest green plastic canvas (page 47). Cut five 52-hole x 3-hole pieces from clear plastic canvas for flowers.

2. Stitch background with sandstone and camel; do not Overcast. Stitch and Overcast frame pieces.

3. Use photo as a guide through step 8. Using hand-sewing needle and blue thread, stitch frame sides to background, then stitch frame top and bottom pieces to background and frame sides.

4. Stitch and Overcast basket and handle. Using hand-sewing needle throughout, use white thread to sew white pearl buttons to basket; using blue thread, center and sew side and bottom edges of basket to lower portion of camel stitches on background. Stitch center of handle to background; tuck handle ends inside basket and tack in place.

5. Stitch and Overcast leaves. Continental Stitch three flowers with lemon; Overcast long edges with yellow and short edges with lemon. Continental Stitch remaining two flowers with pink; Overcast long edges with lavender and short edges with pink.

6. Roll up each flower, then tack together in several places with matching thread. Using white thread, stitch one pearl bead into center of each flower.

7. Using sewing needle and matching thread, stitch leaves then flowers to background.

8. Sew one flower button to each corner of frame; sew butterfly button to basket handle. Insert pearl sprays between leaves and behind flowers; tack to background with needle and thread.

9. Sew sawtooth hanger to top center back of background. ●

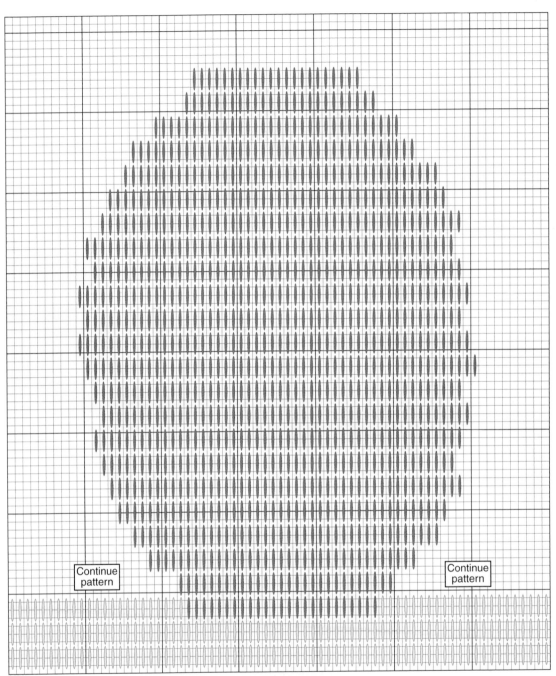

Continue
pattern

Continue
pattern

Flower Basket Background
70 holes x 82 holes
Cut 1 from almond

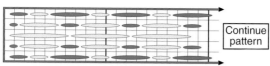

Flower Basket Frame Side
85 holes x 5 holes
Cut 2 from country blue

**Flower Basket
Frame Top & Bottom**
73 holes x 5 holes
Cut 2 from country blue

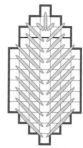

Flower Basket Leaf
7 holes x 13 holes
Cut 5 from forest green

Flower Basket Handle
90 holes x 3 holes
Cut 1 from country blue

COLOR KEY	
Plastic Canvas Yarn	**Yards**
Pink #07	9
Lemon #20	13
Sandstone #16	29
Christmas green #28	5
Royal #32	28
Sail blue #35	18
Camel #43	31
Lavender #05 Overcasting	3
✎ Forest #29 Overcasting	5
Yellow #57 Overcasting	4
○ Attach white pearl button	

Color numbers given are for Uniek Needloft plastic canvas yarn.

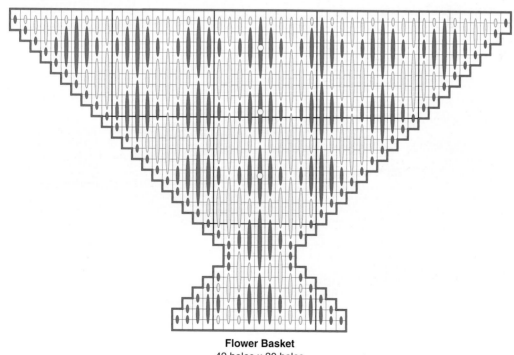

Flower Basket
49 holes x 30 holes
Cut 1 from country blue

Midnight Violets Eyeglasses Case

Enjoy those warm spring evenings out on the town with this shimmering floral accent!

DESIGN BY ALIDA MACOR

Skill Level
Beginner

Size
3¼ inches W x 6½ inches H

Materials
- ½ sheet soft 7-count plastic canvas
- Worsted weight yarn as listed in color key
- Darice metallic cord as listed in color key
- #16 tapestry needle
- Black self-adhesive felt (optional)

Instructions

1. Cut and stitch plastic canvas according to graph, working uncoded background with black Continental Stitches.

2. If using black felt for lining, cut felt one hole smaller than case all around; adhere felt to wrong side.

3. Using black throughout, Overcast top edge from dot to dot. Fold case in half with wrong sides together, then Whipstitch around side and bottom edges, working two stitches per hole for better coverage. ●

COLOR KEY

Worsted Weight Yarn	Yards
■ Violet	4
■ Medium green	3
☐ Bright yellow	2
Uncoded background is Black Continental Stitches	26

Metallic Cord

	Yards
☐ Green/silver #3412-19	4
☐ Lavender/silver #3412-21	3

Color numbers given are for Darice metallic cord.

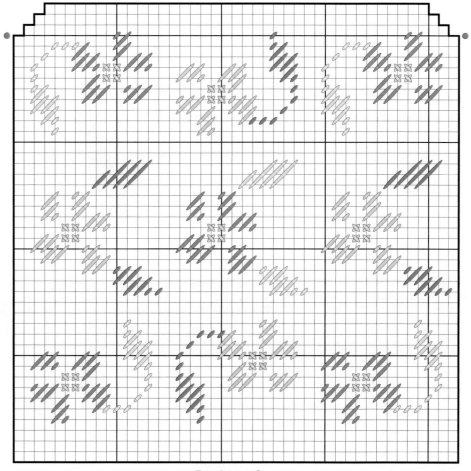

Eyeglasses Case
43 holes x 43 holes
Cut 1

Summer

With golden sunshine filling the days and fireflies lighting the nights, there are few things sweeter than summer's simple pleasures! In this chapter you'll find a fantastic selection of summer projects to capture those moments of "fun in the sun!"

Cute As a Bug Dresser Set

Oh-so-cute and irresistibly friendly, this adorable set makes a lively accent!

DESIGNS BY SUSAN LEINBERGER

Project Note

Use #16 tapestry needle with yarn and #20 tapestry needle with pearl cotton.

Vanity Tray

1. Cut base and sides from plastic canvas according to graphs (pages 52 and 53). Cut adhesive-backed felt to fit base.
2. Stitch pieces following graphs, working uncoded areas with yellow Continental Stitches.
3. When background stitching on base is completed, work black yarn French Knots on ladybugs with full strand; use 1-ply yellow to work French Knots in flower centers. Work black pearl cotton Backstitches and Running Stitches.
4. Cut two 10½-inch lengths and two 7½-inch lengths from red grosgrain ribbon. Center and glue ribbon to wrong sides of tray sides with tacky glue.
5. Whipstitch long sides to short sides with yellow. Using red, Whipstitch sides to base with right side of base facing up; Overcast top edges.
6. Hot-glue four ⅝-inch ladybug buttons to inside corners of tray (see photo).
7. Adhere adhesive-backed felt to bottom of base.

Ladybug Mirror Holder

1. Use emery board to roughen surface of brads. Paint brads with foam brush and red paint, using as many coats as necessary for even, complete coverage; allow to dry thoroughly between coats.
2. Cut front, back and wings from plastic canvas according to graphs (page 52). Cut two 41-hole x 2-hole pieces for holder long sides and two 6-hole x 2-hole

pieces for holder short sides.
3. Continental Stitch sides with black. Stitch back and front following graphs, working uncoded areas with yellow Continental Stitches. Overcast inside edges on front.
4. Work embroidery on back following step 3 under vanity tray.
5. Stitch and Overcast wings, working one as graphed; reverse remaining wing and work stitches in opposite direction. On both wings, work black yarn Wound Cross for ladybug spots following diagram given (page 52).
6. Center and glue mirror to wrong side of holder back. Using black, Whipstitch long sides to short sides, then with mirror side up, Whipstitch back to sides.
7. Insert painted brads through holes on wings where indicated on graph. Fasten wings to front by inserting through holes indicated on front.
8. Whipstitch mirror front to mirror sides with black. Hot-glue cabochons to front for eyes.

Brush Cover

1. Cut top and side from plastic canvas according to graphs (pages 52 and 53).
2. Stitch pieces following graphs, working uncoded areas with yellow Continental Stitches.
3. Work embroidery on top following step 3 under vanity tray.
4. Using yellow throughout, Whipstitch side to top around side and top edges from arrow to arrow; Overcast remaining edges. Work pearl cotton Running Stitches on side.
5. Hot-glue assembled brush cover to

Skill Level

Intermediate

Size

Vanity Tray: 11 inches W x ⅝ inches H x 7⅞ inches D
Mirror Holder: Fits oval mirror 3 inches W x 5 inches L
Brush Cover: Fits brush, including handle, 1⅛ inches W x 6 inches L
Comb Cover: Fits 5-inch comb

Materials

- 2 sheets 7-count plastic canvas
- Uniek Needloft plastic canvas yarn as listed in color key
- #3 pearl cotton as listed in color key
- #16 tapestry needle
- #20 tapestry needle
- Red acrylic craft paint to match yarn
- Small foam paintbrush
- Emery board
- 2 (⁵⁄₁₆-inch-wide x ¾-inch-long) paper brads
- 1⅓ yards ¾-inch-wide red grosgrain ribbon
- ⅜-inch ladybug button
- 4 (⅝-inch) ladybug buttons
- 2 (7mm) round black cabochons
- 3-inch x 5-inch oval mirror
- 1⅛-inch-wide x 6-inch-long hair brush (including handle)
- 5-inch comb
- 1 sheet red adhesive-backed felt
- Tacky craft glue
- Hot-glue gun

back of brush. Tie remaining length of ribbon in a bow around handle next to cover; trim tails as desired.

Comb Cover

1. Cut sides from plastic canvas according to graph. Cut one 40-hole x 2-hole piece for cover top.

2. Stitch top with yellow Continental Stitches. Stitch sides following graph. When background stitching is completed, use 1-ply yellow to work French Knots in flower centers.

3. Using yellow throughout, Whipstitch sides to top around side and top edges from arrow to arrow; Overcast remaining edges.

4. Work black pearl cotton running stitches on sides.

5. Hot-glue small ladybug button to one side of comb cover (see photo). Glue comb inside cover. ●

Vanity Tray Long Side
71 holes x 4 holes
Cut 2

Vanity Tray Short Side
51 holes x 4 holes
Cut 2

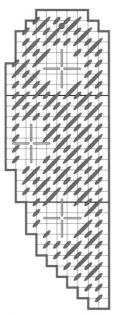

Ladybug Mirror Holder Wing
10 holes x 28 holes
Cut 2
Stitch 1 as graphed
Reverse 1 and work stitches
in opposite direction

A **B**

Wound Cross

Following graph A, work 4 Straight Stitches, coming up at 1, down in the center, up at 3, down in the center, etc. Following graph B, bring yarn up at arrow, then wind yarn under all Straight Stitches, ending where shown.

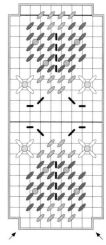

Brush Cover Top
9 holes x 21 holes
Cut 1

Comb Cover Side
35 holes x 3 holes
Cut 2

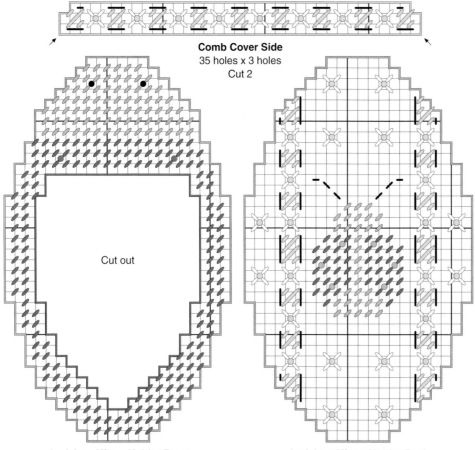

Cut out

Ladybug Mirror Holder Front
22 holes x 36 holes
Cut 1

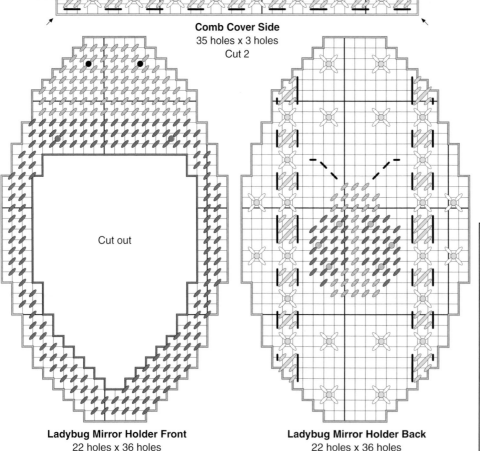

Ladybug Mirror Holder Back
22 holes x 36 holes
Cut 1

COLOR KEY
Plastic Canvas Yarn   Yarn
■ Black #00
■ Red #01
☐ White #41
☐ Yellow #57
   Uncoded areas are yellow
   #57 Continental Stitches
╱ Black #00 Wound Cross
● Black #00 (2-ply) French Knot
○ Yellow #57 (1-ply) French Knot
#3 Pearl Cotton
╱ Black Backstitch and
   Running Stitch
● Attach brad
● Attach cabochon
Color numbers given are for Uniek Needloft
plastic canvas yarn.

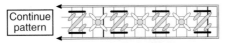

Brush Cover Side
51 holes x 3 holes
Cut 1

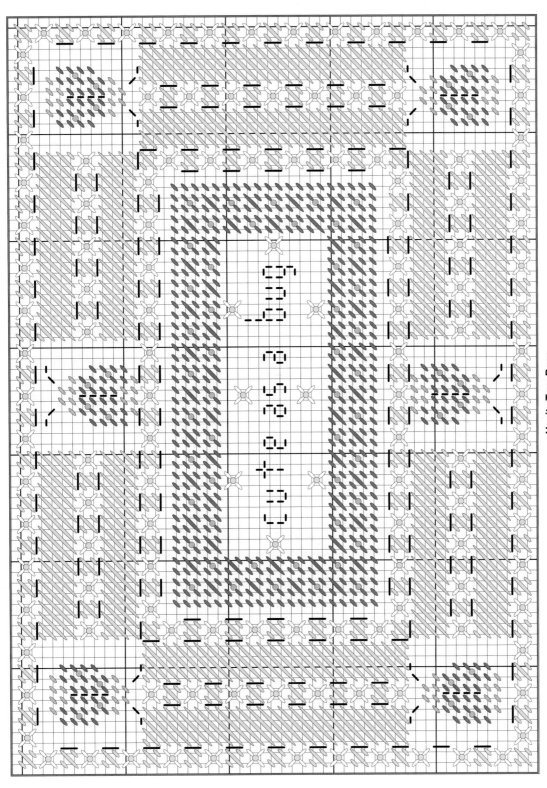

Vanity Tray Base
71 holes x 51 holes
Cut 1

Island Paradise

If you're dreaming of palm trees and warm sandy beaches, this fanciful project brings the tropics to you!

DESIGN BY ROBIN HOWARD WILL

Skill Level
Beginner

Size
7 inches W x 11¾ inches H

Materials
- 1 sheet 7-count plastic canvas
- Uniek Needloft plastic canvas yarn as listed in color key
- Raffia straw as listed in color key
- Twine as listed in color key
- #16 tapestry needle
- 5mm black cabochon
- 7-inch length magnet strip
- Hot-glue gun

Project Note

f twine is too thick to thread through needle, pull fibers apart to make it thin enough to fit.

Instructions

1. Cut plastic canvas according to graphs.

2. Stitch and Overcast pieces following graphs, working Christmas green Straight Stitches on palm tree leaves and camel Backstitches on tree trunk when background stitching is completed.

3. Using photo as a guide, glue eye and wing to flamingo. Glue coconuts to palm tree. Glue flamingo beak and bottom of neck to trunk of tree.

4. Cut magnet strip into one 3-inch and two 2-inch lengths. Glue 3-inch length to wrong side of tree trunk. Glue 2-inch lengths to wrong sides of flamingo body and palm tree leaves. ●

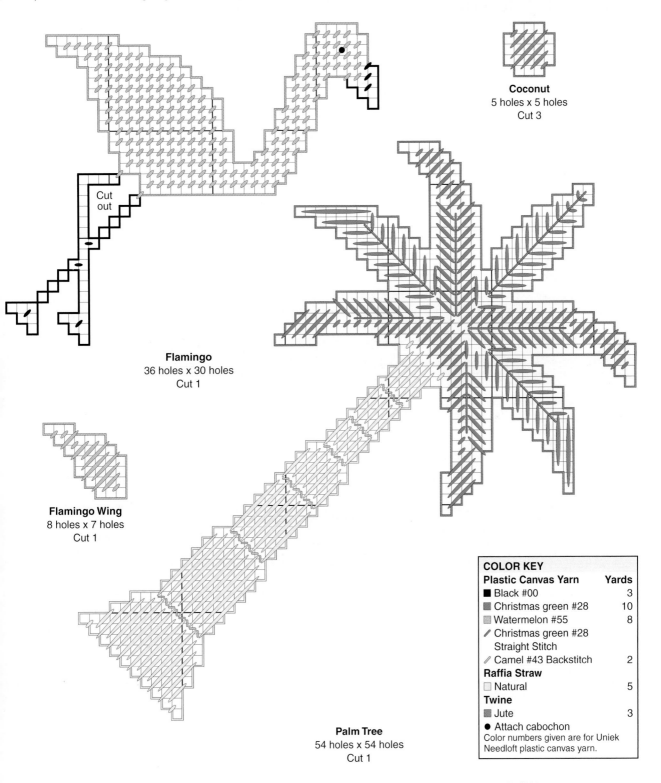

Coconut
5 holes x 5 holes
Cut 3

Flamingo
36 holes x 30 holes
Cut 1

Flamingo Wing
8 holes x 7 holes
Cut 1

Palm Tree
54 holes x 54 holes
Cut 1

COLOR KEY	
Plastic Canvas Yarn	**Yards**
■ Black #00	3
■ Christmas green #28	10
□ Watermelon #55	8
╱ Christmas green #28 Straight Stitch	
╱ Camel #43 Backstitch	2
Raffia Straw	
□ Natural	5
Twine	
▨ Jute	3
● Attach cabochon	
Color numbers given are for Uniek Needloft plastic canvas yarn.	

Happy Frog Tote

This flower-bearing frog puckers up with glee at the chance to lend a "hopping" hand!

DESIGN BY JANNA BRITTON

Skill Level
Intermediate

Size
9¹⁄₈ inches W x 11 inches H x 1¼ inches D

Materials
- 2 sheets bright green Uniek QuickCount 7-count plastic canvas
- ½ sheet clear 7-count plastic canvas
- Uniek Needloft plastic canvas yarn as listed in color key
- #16 tapestry needle
- 6 (5mm) yellow pompoms
- ½-inch yellow pompom
- 2 (20mm) movable eyes
- ¾ inch 1-inch-wide hook-and-loop tape
- Low-temperature glue gun

Cutting & Stitching

1. Cut two frog bodies, one set of eyelids, two handles, two sides, one arms piece and one base from bright green plastic canvas; cut three flower pieces and one lips piece from clear plastic canvas according to graphs (this page and page 58). One handle will remain unstitched.

2. Stitch and Overcast arms, lips and flower pieces following graphs. Stitch one handle, leaving four bars on each end unworked.

3. Stitch remaining pieces following graphs, working back in fern Mosaic Stitch pattern only, eliminating all embroidery.

4. When background stitching is completed on front, work holly Backstitches to detail legs and feet; using black, work Backstitches for nose and Outline Stitch (page 58) for mouth.

Assembly

1. Use holly through step 3 unless otherwise instructed. Overcast inside edges of eyelids from dot to dot, then match remaining edges to eyelid edges on frog front and Whipstitch together. Glue eyes in place.

2. Leaving bottom edges between arrows unworked on both front and back, Overcast back and remaining edges of front.

3. Using photo as a guide through step 9, tack shoulders of arms in place to frog front where indicated with blue lines. Using watermelon, tack lips to front in pink shaded area.

4. Using fern, Overcast top edges of sides; Whipstitch bottom edges of sides to side edges of base. Using holly, Whipstitch remaining edges of base to front and back between arrows.

5. Using fern throughout, stitch sides to front and back along red lines by duplicating stitches in Mosaic Stitch pattern; Overcast edges of sides that show between head and legs.

6. Using white, tack flower pieces together in center, overlapping petals as needed, then tack to center of arms. Glue large yellow pompom to center of flower.

7. Glue 5mm yellow pompoms to knees for freckles.

8. Using fern, Whipstitch two handle pieces together. Duplicating some stitches in Mosaic Stitch pattern, attach unworked ends securely in place on inside of tote front and back in green shaded area on graph.

9. Glue adhesive backed hook-and-loop tape to handle ends. **Note:** *Using glue adds extra stability.* ●

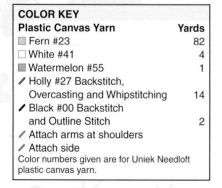

Frog Tote Lips
6 holes x 6 holes
Cut 1 from clear

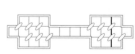

Frog Tote Flower
12 holes x 3 holes
Cut 3 from clear

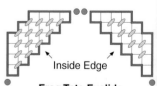

Inside Edge

Frog Tote Eyelids
6 holes x 6 holes each
Cut 1 set from bright green

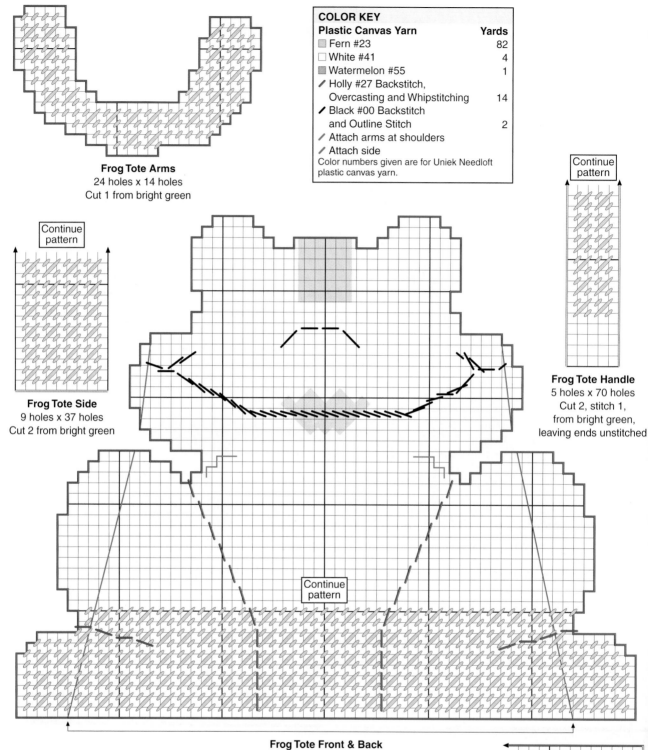

Frog Tote Arms
24 holes x 14 holes
Cut 1 from bright green

COLOR KEY

Plastic Canvas Yarn		Yards
☐ Fern #23		82
☐ White #41		4
☐ Watermelon #55		1
⁄ Holly #27 Backstitch, Overcasting and Whipstitching		14
⁄ Black #00 Backstitch and Outline Stitch		2
⁄ Attach arms at shoulders		
⁄ Attach side		

Color numbers given are for Uniek Needloft plastic canvas yarn.

Continue pattern

Frog Tote Side
9 holes x 37 holes
Cut 2 from bright green

Continue pattern

Frog Tote Handle
5 holes x 70 holes
Cut 2, stitch 1,
from bright green,
leaving ends unstitched

Continue pattern

Frog Tote Front & Back
60 holes x 47 holes
Cut 2 from bright green
Stitch front as graphed
Stitch back with fern Mosaic Stitch pattern only

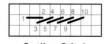

Outline Stitch
Bring needle up at 1, down at 2,
up at 3, down at 4, etc.

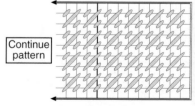

Continue pattern

Frog Tote Base
49 holes x 9 holes
Cut 1 from bright green

Ladybug Dreams Journal

These delightful ladybugs live on a log—a daily log, that is! Along with their pen-topper pal, they will encourage your thoughts to flourish!

DESIGN BY JANNA BRITTON

Instructions

1. Cut plastic canvas according to graphs (pages 60 and 61). Cut two 4-hole x 42-hole pieces for inner straps. Straps will remain unstitched.

2. Stitch and Overcast ladybug pen topper, then stitch remaining pieces following graphs, working uncoded areas with white Continental Stitches. Do not work embroidery at this time.

3. Using white yarn, Overcast three outside edges on both cover front and back from black dot to black dot, Whipstitching unworked inner straps to top and bottom edges where indicated on graphs while Overcasting. Overcast top and bottom edges of spine.

4. Work black pearl cotton embroidery on ladybug pen topper and two large ladybugs on cover front. Work all remaining embroidery with 6-strand embroidery floss.

5. Using white yarn, Whipstitch spine to front and back.

6. Glue movable eyes to ladybug pen topper and two large ladybugs on cover front where indicated on graphs.

7. Insert covers of spiral-bound notebook between straps and cover pieces.

8. Attach ladybug pen topper to cap of pen with two black pearl cotton stitches around cap, working through yarn on back of piece; secure with glue. ●

Skill Level

Beginner

Size

4⅝ inches W x 6⅜ inches H x ⅞ inches D (fits 4-inch x 6-inch spiral-bound notebook)

Materials

- 1 sheet 7-count plastic canvas
- Uniek Needloft plastic canvas yarn as listed in color key
- #3 pearl cotton as listed in color key
- DMC 6-strand embroidery floss as listed in color key
- #16 tapestry needle
- 6 (4mm) movable eyes
- 4-inch x 6-inch spiral-bound notebook
- Red ink pen with cap
- Hot-glue gun

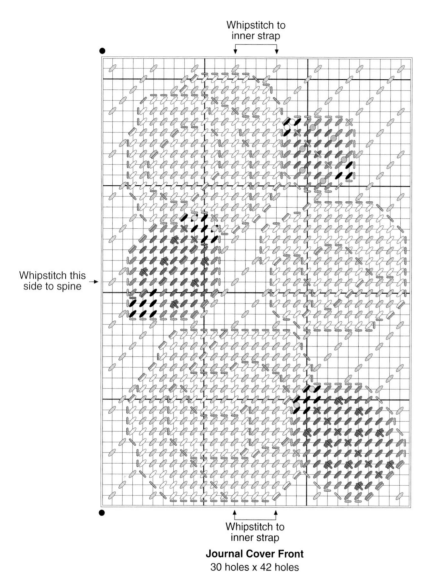

Whipstitch to
inner strap

Whipstitch this
side to spine

Whipstitch to
inner strap

Journal Cover Front
30 holes x 42 holes
Cut 1

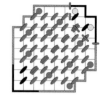

Ladybug Pen Topper
8 holes x 8 holes
Cut 1

COLOR KEY	
Plastic Canvas Yarn	**Yards**
■ Black #00	1
▨ Red #01	5
▤ Christmas red #02	5
☐ Lemon #20	5
▨ Fern #23	12
▨ Yellow #57	8
Uncoded areas are white	
#41 Continental Stitches	28
⁄ White Overcasting	
and Whipstitching	
#3 Pearl Cotton	
⁄ Black Backstitch	2
✖ Black Cross Stitch	
● Black French Knot	
6-Strand Embroidery Floss	
⁄ Lemon #307 Backstitch	5
⁄ Black #310 Backstitch	2
○ White French Knot	1
● Black #310 French Knot	
○ Attach movable eye	
Color numbers given are for Uniek Needloft	
plastic canvas yarn and DMC 6-strand	
embroidery floss.	

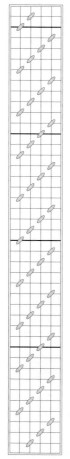

Journal Cover Spine
5 holes x 42 holes
Cut 1

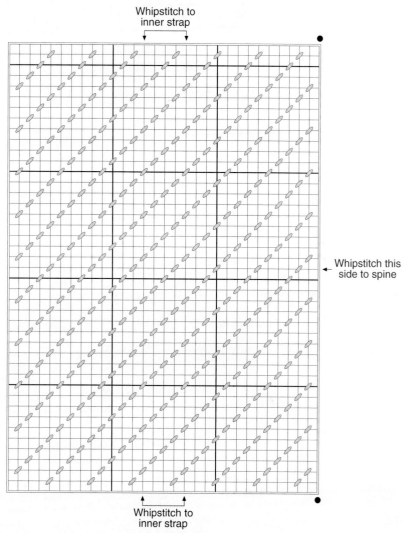

Whipstitch to
inner strap

Whipstitch this
side to spine

Whipstitch to
inner strap

Journal Cover Back
30 holes x 42 holes
Cut 1

Flower Vendor Centerpiece

This perky bumblebee and his turtle companion bring bouquets of flowers to brighten any room.

DESIGN BY JANELLE GIESE

Project Notes

The triangle, heart, square, inverted triangle and diamond shapes designate Continental Stitches.

When stitching base sides, do not draw threads over Whipstitch lines on back of each piece.

Dowel & Wire Pole

1. Glue one end of dowel in and through hole of wooden wheel so end of dowel and side of wheel are flush, making the wheel the base for the dowel.

2. For wire pole, bend one end of wire into a small loop, then bend wire into a slight arch.

3. Following manufacturer's directions, paint and seal dowel and wire, allowing to dry thoroughly before applying sealer.

Cutting & Stitching

1. Cut plastic canvas according to graphs (pages 64 and 65). Cut one 24-hole x 24-hole piece for base bottom.

2. Place both inner base pieces together and stitch as one; Overcast inside edges. Continental Stitch base bottom with dark sage.

3. Leaving red line and blue highlighted areas unworked at this time, stitch base sides, working uncoded area around flowers with off-white Continental Stitches; work one side as graphed and one each replacing orange (front) with grenadine (right side), cherry red (back) and periwinkle (left side).

4. Stitch grape pieces and vendor front and back following graphs. Overcast bottom edges of front and back from red dot

to red dot, using dark sage for turtle's legs and lime for shell.

5. Using a full strand yarn, Straight Stitch eyes with black and embroider features on basket with mid brown.

6. Work pearl braid embroidery on grape pieces and for bee's wings and flower centers, working Straight Stitches for bee's wings in opposite direction of background stitches first, then work top layer in same direction as Continental Stitches.

7. For Pin Stitches on eyes, bring pearl braid up in hole indicated above black Straight Stitch, bring down through black yarn, splitting stitch and going back through same hole in which stitch originated.

8. Complete embroidery with pearl cotton, working Backstitches, Straight Stitches and Lazy Daisy Stitches following color key and graphs.

9. For each antenna, form one knot at the end of a length of black pearl cotton. Bring needle from front to back where indicated on graph, leaving end with knot on front, allowing length to be about ³⁄₄-inch-long; anchor on backside. Stiffen antennae with glue between fingers.

Assembly

1. Working counter clockwise and with front facing up, Whipstitch wrong sides of front and back together, beginning at lower right red dot, around side and top edges to lower left red dot.

2. Whipstitch inner base to base sides along red lines, working Continental and Slanted Gobelin Stitches as graphed. After inner base is attached to sides, use

Skill Level

Advanced

Size

7½ inches W x 15 inches H x 3¾ inches D

Materials

- 2⅓ sheets 7-count plastic canvas
- Coats & Clark Red Heart Classic worsted weight yarn Art. E267 as listed in color key
- Coats & Clark Red Heart Super Saver worsted weight yarn Art. E300 as listed in color key
- Coats & Clark Red Heart Kids worsted weight yarn Art. E711 as listed in color key
- Kreinik Tapestry (#12) Braid as listed in color key
- DMC #3 pearl cotton as listed in color key
- DMC #5 pearl cotton: 1 yard white and as listed in color key
- #16 tapestry needle
- 12 inches ¼-inch wooden dowel
- 1¾-inch wooden wheel
- 5 inches 18-gauge steel wire
- Ivory acrylic craft paint
- Small paintbrush
- Spray sealer
- ¾ cup aquarium gravel
- Needle-nose pliers
- Thick white glue

dark sage to Whipstitch sides together; Overcast top edges.

3. Insert dowel up through opening in inner base until wheel meets wrong side of inner base. Whipstitch base bottom to bottom edges of base sides, filling with aquarium gravel before closing.

4. Whipstitch grape pieces together with purple. Cut white pearl cotton in half. Using one length for "rope," knot one end and draw up through grape and out top, pulling knot to inside. Tie remaining length in a bow around rope at top of grape.

5. Insert straight end of wire pole between front and back at arrow. Thread pearl cotton rope through loop of pole and tie in a knot, adjusting length as desired. Trim ends of knot.

6. Apply a dab of glue behind bow, knot and where pole inserts into motifs. Apply glue to top end of dowel and insert inside front and back. ●

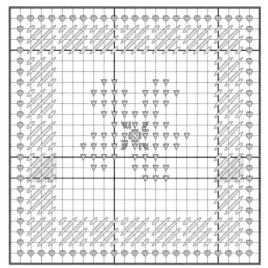

Vendor Base Side
24 holes x 24 holes
Cut 4
Stitch 1 as graphed
Stitch one each, replacing orange with grenadine, cherry red and light periwinkle

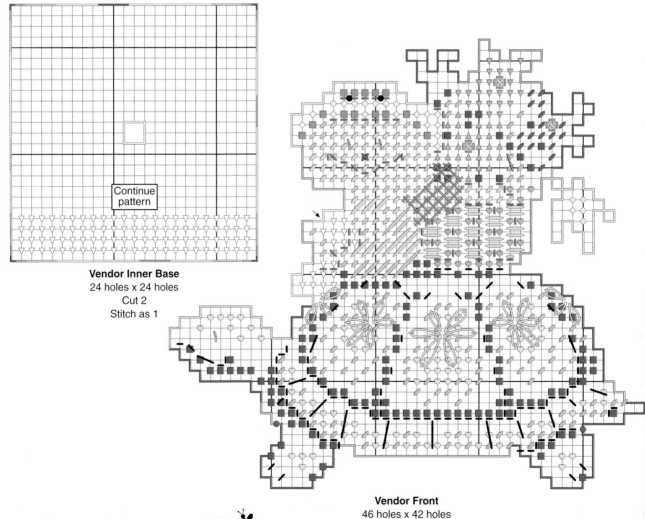

Vendor Inner Base
24 holes x 24 holes
Cut 2
Stitch as 1

Continue pattern

Vendor Front
46 holes x 42 holes
Cut 1

Vendor Grape
5 holes x 6 holes
Cut 2

Vendor Back
46 holes x 42 holes
Cut 1

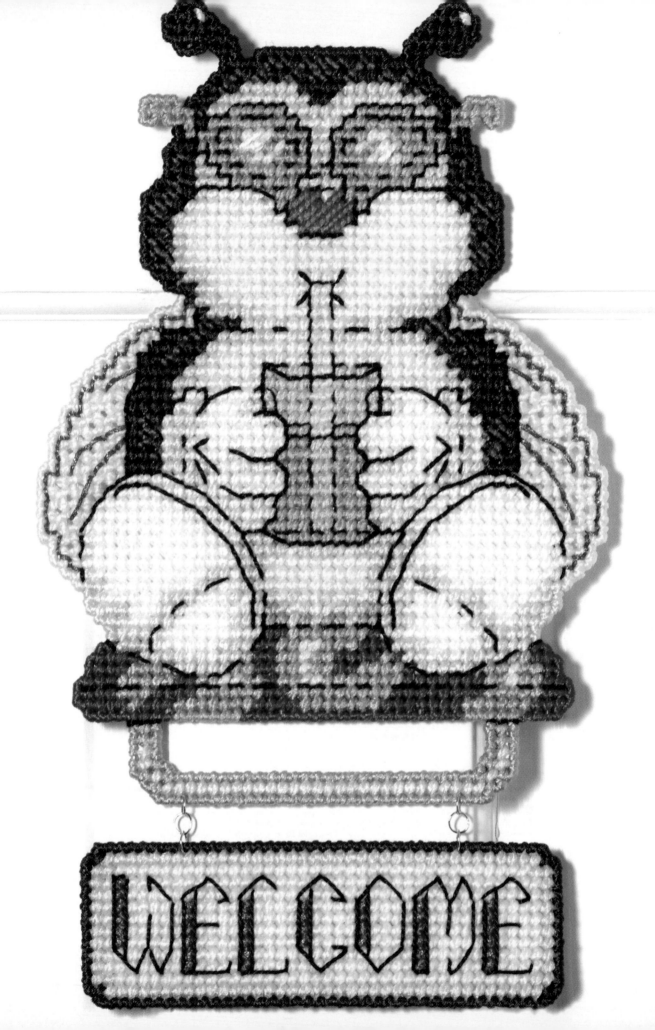

Summer Bug Welcome

This clever critter knows how to stay cool as he cheerfully welcomes your guests!

DESIGN BY JANELLE GIESE

Project Notes

The triangle, heart, square, inverted triangle and diamond shapes designate Continental Stitches.

The sign graph is shared with the other bug welcome designs in other chapters of this book. Colors used for each season are given with the graphs and/or the instructions for that season.

Instructions

1. Cut bug (page 68) and sign (page 34) from plastic canvas according to graphs.

2. Stitch and Overcast welcome sign following graph, working uncoded background with eggshell Continental Stitches; replace lavender yarn with red yarn.

3. When background stitching on sign is completed, work red heavy braid Straight Stitches over red yarn Continental Stitches. Using black #3 pearl cotton, embroider remaining portions of lettering.

4. Stitch and Overcast bug, working uncoded areas with baby yellow Continental Stitches.

5. When background stitching is completed, use a full strand white yarn to Straight Stitch eye and antennae highlights; use 1-ply tangerine to work Straight Stitches over silver yarn thumbs.

6. Backstitch red heavy braid accents on wings. Use black #5 pearl cotton to work Straight Stitches over red yarn Continental Stitches and embroidery detailing straw and a small portion of glass. Use black #3 pearl cotton for all remaining embroidery.

7. Sew sawtooth hanger to top center back of bug's head with #5 pearl cotton. Using needle-nose pliers, join bug to sign by forming two chains of three jump rings each, attaching top and bottom jump rings through holes indicated with green dots. ●

Skill Level

Advanced

Size

7½ inches W x 12½ inches H

Materials

- 1 sheet stiff 7-count plastic canvas
- Uniek Needloft plastic canvas yarn as listed in color key
- Kreinik Heavy (#32) Braid as listed in color key
- #5 pearl cotton as listed in color key
- #3 pearl cotton as listed in color key
- #16 tapestry needle
- Sawtooth hanger
- 6 (7mm) nickel jump rings
- Needle-nose pliers

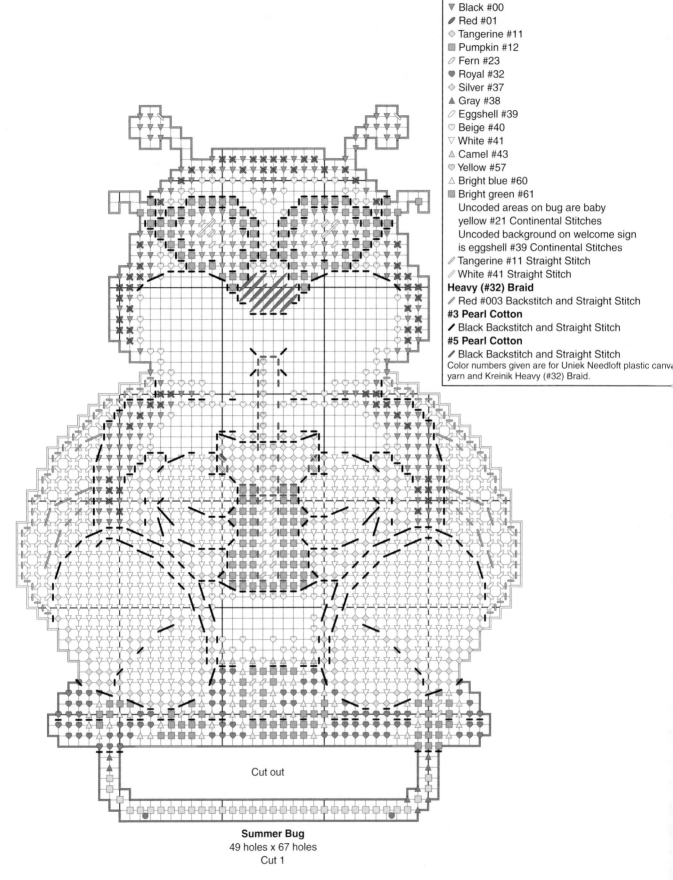

COLOR KEY

Plastic Canvas Yarn

▽ Black #00
⬖ Red #01
◇ Tangerine #11
▣ Pumpkin #12
⬗ Fern #23
♥ Royal #32
◇ Silver #37
▲ Gray #38
⬗ Eggshell #39
♡ Beige #40
▽ White #41
△ Camel #43
♡ Yellow #57
△ Bright blue #60
▣ Bright green #61
   Uncoded areas on bug are baby
   yellow #21 Continental Stitches
   Uncoded background on welcome sign
   is eggshell #39 Continental Stitches
⟋ Tangerine #11 Straight Stitch
⟋ White #41 Straight Stitch

Heavy (#32) Braid
⟋ Red #003 Backstitch and Straight Stitch

#3 Pearl Cotton
⟋ Black Backstitch and Straight Stitch

#5 Pearl Cotton
⟋ Black Backstitch and Straight Stitch

Color numbers given are for Uniek Needloft plastic canv_
yarn and Kreinik Heavy (#32) Braid.

Cut out

Summer Bug
49 holes x 67 holes
Cut 1

Flutterbugs Puppets

The spirit of summer lies right at your fingertips when you stitch these glittering glove puppets!

DESIGNS BY JANNA BRITTON

Skill Level

Intermediate

Size

Butterfly: 10¼ inches W x 7 inches H, excluding glove

Dragonfly: 6½ inches W x 5⅜ inches H, excluding glove

Materials

Each Puppet

- #16 tapestry needle
- ¼-inch-wide double-sided adhesive tape
- 1 child-size yellow garden glove
- Low-temperature glue gun

Butterfly

- 2 (6-inch) Uniek QuickShape plastic canvas hearts
- ¼ sheet black 7-count plastic canvas
- ⅜-inch-wide curling ribbon as listed in color key
- 2 (5mm) yellow pompoms
- Sewing needle
- Black carpet thread

Dragonfly

- ½ sheet Uniek QuickCount bright purple 7-count plastic canvas
- ³⁄₁₆-inch-wide curling ribbon as listed in color key
- ½-inch lime pompom
- 2 (5mm) movable eyes

Project Notes

Use ⅜-inch-wide ribbon for butterfly and ³⁄₁₆-inch-wide ribbon for dragonfly. Keep curling ribbon smooth and flat while stitching.

To keep backs of pieces looking neat, when ending one ribbon, trim to ½ inch or less, adhere to new ribbon piece with double-sided adhesive tape and repeat last stitch to cover overlap as needed, or simply hold in place on back over a previous stitch with double-sided adhesive tape.

Instructions

1. Cut plastic canvas according to graphs, cutting away gray area on plastic canvas hearts and cutting away blue lines in antennae area on butterfly body.

2. For butterfly, stitch body with black. Stitch wings, beginning with yellow flower and lime green leaves, working Straight Stitches in center of leaves last. Work center of flowers with lavender, following Double Leviathan Stitch diagram.

3. Continue with wings by stitching large pink hearts and small lavender hearts, then stitch background in purple.

4. Using yellow, Whipstitch cut edge of wings to body sides where indicated on graph, Overcasting remaining edges of wings while Whipstitching.

5. Using sewing needle and black carpet thread, stitch body to top of center finger on glove. Glue one yellow pompom to end of each antenna.

6. For dragonfly, stitch body with bright pink and yellow, following the Herringbone Stitch Variation diagram; stitch tail with lavender Straight Stitches.

7. Beginning at wing tips, stitch wings with lavender, following with lime green, yellow, bright pink, then lavender at the base; work lavender Straight Stitch last.

8. Whipstitch base on wings to both sides of body were indicated, leaving all other edges unworked.

9. Glue lime pompom to head of body; glue movable eyes to pompom. Glue dragonfly body to middle finger of glove. ●

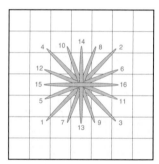

Double Leviathan Stitch
Work stitches in order given, coming up at 1, down at 2, up at 3, down at 4, etc.

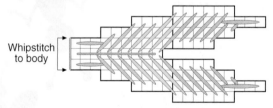

Dragonfly Puppet Wing
19 holes x 9 holes
Cut 2 from bright purple
Stitch with ³⁄₁₆-inch-wide ribbon

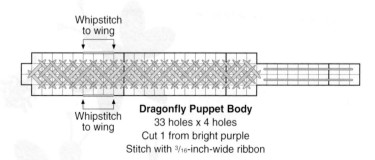

Dragonfly Puppet Body
33 holes x 4 holes
Cut 1 from bright purple
Stitch with ³⁄₁₆-inch-wide ribbon

COLOR KEY	
⅜-Inch-Wide Curling Ribbon	**Yards**
■ Purple	17
□ Yellow	6
□ Bright pink	4
□ Lime green	4
■ Black	3
□ Lavender	2
╱ Lime green Straight Stitch	
³⁄₁₆-Inch-Wide Curling Ribbon	
□ Bright pink	3
□ Yellow	3
□ Lavender	2
□ Lime green	1
╱ Lavender Straight Stitch	

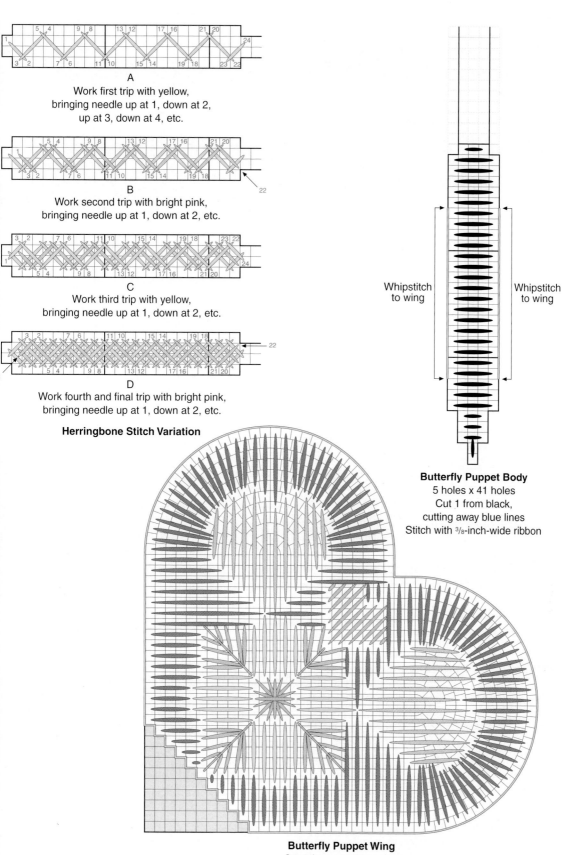

A

Work first trip with yellow,
bringing needle up at 1, down at 2,
up at 3, down at 4, etc.

B

Work second trip with bright pink,
bringing needle up at 1, down at 2, etc.

C

Work third trip with yellow,
bringing needle up at 1, down at 2, etc.

D

Work fourth and final trip with bright pink,
bringing needle up at 1, down at 2, etc.

Herringbone Stitch Variation

Whipstitch
to wing

Whipstitch
to wing

Butterfly Puppet Body
5 holes x 41 holes
Cut 1 from black,
cutting away blue lines
Stitch with ³⁄₈-inch-wide ribbon

Butterfly Puppet Wing
Cut 2 from plastic canvas
heart shapes,
cutting away gray area
Stitch with ³⁄₈-inch-wide ribbon

Luminescent Candlesticks

Regal and refined, these gorgeous adornments capture the glow of a warm summer evening!

DESIGNS BY JANELLE GIESE

Skill Level
Advanced

Size
Day: 5³⁄₈ inches W x 14⁷⁄₈ inches H x 3¹⁄₈ inches D
Night: 5³⁄₄ inches W x 14⁷⁄₈ inches H x 3¹⁄₈ inches D

Materials
- ½ sheet stiff 7-count plastic canvas
- 1¼ sheets regular 7-count plastic canvas
- Uniek Needloft plastic canvas yarn as listed in color key
- Kreinik Heavy (#32) Braid as listed in color key
- DMC #5 pearl cotton as listed in color key
- #16 tapestry needle
- 2 (12-inch) lengths ¼-inch wooden dowel
- 2 (1¾-inch) toy wooden wheels
- 2 (1³⁄₈-inch x 1⁵⁄₈-inch) wooden candle cups with brass inserts
- Small amount antique white felt
- 16 inches 24-gauge green florist's wire
- Pencil
- 1¹⁄₈ cups aquarium gravel
- Ivory acrylic craft paint
- Spray sealer
- Paintbrush
- ¼-inch drill bit
- Drill
- Needle-nose pliers
- 2 drip protectors (optional)
- Thick white glue

Wooden Pieces
1. For each candlestick, glue one end of dowel in and through hole of wooden wheel so end of dowel and side of wheel are flush, making the wheel the base for the candlestick.
2. Drill hole in base of each candle cup to ¼ inch. Lightly place candle cups on opposite ends of dowel to hold for painting; they will be attached later.
3. Following manufacturer's directions, paint and seal each candlestick assembly; allow to dry thoroughly.
4. Remove candle cups. Place one brass insert in each completed cup; set aside.

Cutting & Stitching
1. Cut one each of day and night motifs from stiff plastic canvas (pages 74 and 75); cut all remaining pieces (pages 74 and 75) from regular plastic canvas according to graphs. Base bottoms will remain unstitched.
2. Cut two pieces of felt slightly smaller all around than base bottoms; set aside.
3. Stitch and Overcast day and night motifs and leaves following graphs, working uncoded areas on day motif with eggshell Continental Stitches and uncoded areas on night motif with gray Continental Stitches.
4. Stitch caps; Overcast edges, Whipstitching darts closed on each. Stitch base top and sides.
5. When Background stitching and Overcasting are completed, work pearl cotton embroidery on day and night motifs and leaves, working Half Cross Stitches with ultra dark beaver gray over gray Continental Stitches on day motif first.

5. Work gold braid embroidery next, placing ends of two stitches on back of day motif where indicated with green dot.
6. Using 1-ply eggshell, Straight Stitch antennae and highlights of abdomen on night motif.
7. Using eggshell, Whipstitch base tops to base sides where indicated on graphs. For each base, Whipstitch five top/side pieces together with moss and eggshell. Do not Overcast top edges as fit will be snug.
8. Work gold braid embroidery around base sides, stitching over corners as indicated.

Assembly
1. Insert dowel up through opening at very top (tip) of base until wheel meets stitching on inside of base. ***Note:*** *There will be space between wheel and tip.* Using moss, Whipstitch base bottom to base sides, filling firmly with aquarium gravel before closing.
2. For each base, using moss, Whipstitch three cap pieces together at red dots, forming two rings. Slide each ring over top of one dowel to base tip.
3. Apply glue to tops of dowels and press candle cups firmly into place. Apply glue to base tips and undersides of caps; press firmly together; tie with a scrap of yarn to hold until dry.
4. Cut wire into two 6-inch lengths and two 2-inch lengths. For vines, curl each 6-inch length around pencil; bend one end on each in a tiny loop and straighten opposite end slightly.
5. For each leaf, place one end of a 2-inch length wire behind leaf and tack in place with pearl cotton. Bend tip of wire

over tacking point and squeeze to close loop. Add a dab of glue to secure.

6. Using photo as a guide, for each candlestick, glue wire vine and wire leaf stem into ring between cap and dowel. Arrange as desired, then add a dab of glue to bottom tip of each leaf and press into base top. Glue felt to base bottoms.

7. Locate vertical centers on day and night motifs. Using eggshell, Whipstitch one dowel to each motif through stitching on backs of motifs near top and bottom edges; apply dabs of glue to keep motifs from pivoting.

8. If desired, use drip protectors to keep needlework wax free. ●

COLOR KEY

Plastic Canvas Yarn	Yards
▨ Tangerine #11	2
■ Maple #13	2
▨ Sandstone #16	5
▨ Baby yellow #21	4
▨ Moss #25	18
▨ Gray #38	9
☐ Eggshell #39	37
▨ Beige #40	9
▨ Camel #43	2

Uncoded areas on night motif are gray #38 Continental Stitches
Uncoded areas on day motif are eggshell #39 Continental Stitches
⁄ Eggshell #39 Straight Stitch

Heavy (#32) Braid
⁄ Gold #002 Backstitch
and Straight Stitch   10

#5 Pearl Cotton
⁄ Dark beaver gray #646 Backstitch
and Straight Stitch   6
⁄ Ultra dark beaver gray #844 Backstitch,
Straight Stitch and Half Cross Stitch   3

Color numbers given are for Uniek Needloft plastic canvas yarn, Kreinik Heavy (#32) Braid and DMC #5 pearl cotton.

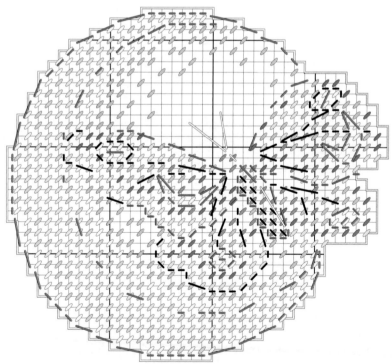

Luminescent Candlestick Night Motif
37 holes x 33 holes
Cut 1 from stiff

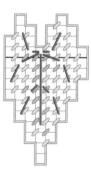

Luminescent Candlesticks Leaf
8 holes x 14 holes
Cut 2 (1 for each base) from regular

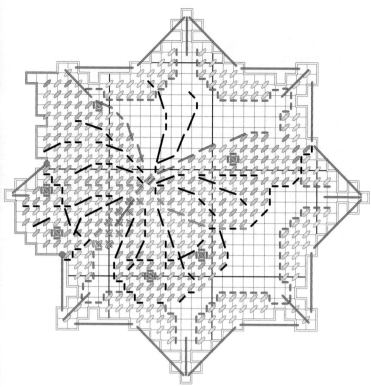

Luminescent Candlestick Day Motif
35 holes x 35 holes
Cut 1 from stiff

Whipstitch to base top

Luminescent Candlesticks
Base Side
13 holes x 7 holes
Cut 10 (5 for each base) from regular

Dart

Luminescent Candlesticks
Base Cap
5 holes x 6 holes
Cut 6 (3 for each base) from regular

COLOR KEY	
Plastic Canvas Yarn	**Yards**
▨ Tangerine #11	2
■ Maple #13	2
▨ Sandstone #16	5
▨ Baby yellow #21	4
▨ Moss #25	18
▨ Gray #38	9
▨ Eggshell #39	37
▨ Beige #40	9
▨ Camel #43	2
Uncoded areas on night motif are gray #38 Continental Stitches	
Uncoded areas on day motif are eggshell #39 Continental Stitches	
╱ Eggshell #39 Straight Stitch	
Heavy (#32) Braid	
╱ Gold #002 Backstitch and Straight Stitch	10
#5 Pearl Cotton	
╱ Dark beaver gray #646 Backstitch and Straight Stitch	6
╱ Ultra dark beaver gray #844 Backstitch, Straight Stitch and Half Cross Stitch	3
Color numbers given are for Uniek Needloft plastic canvas yarn, Kreinik Heavy (#32) Braid and DMC #5 pearl cotton.	

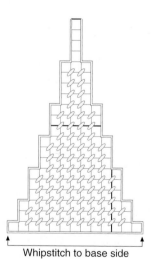

Whipstitch to base side

Luminescent Candlesticks
Base Top
13 holes x 20 holes
Cut 10 (5 for each base) from regular

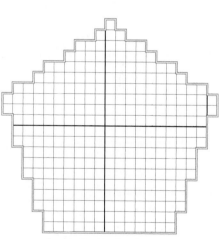

Luminescent Candlesticks
Base Bottom
21 holes x 20 holes
Cut 2 (1 for each base) from regular
Do not stitch

Critter Catcher Kit

Put a new spin on the timeless fun of catching bugs! Our playful design is easy to stitch, and the open mesh canvas makes the perfect critter showcase!

DESIGNS BY SUSAN LEINBERGER

Skill Level

Beginner

Size

Critter Catcher: 5¾ inches W x 16¾ inches L
Critter Corral: 4½ inches W x 5⅛ inches H x 7 inches D

Materials

- 1½ sheets bright purple Uniek QuickCount 7-count plastic canvas
- 1½ sheets clear stiff 7-count plastic canvas
- 2 (6-inch) Uniek QuickShape plastic canvas radial circles
- Uniek Needloft plastic canvas yarn as listed in color key
- Uniek Needloft metallic craft cord as listed in color key
- Uniek Needloft iridescent craft cord as listed in color key
- #16 tapestry needle
- #20 tapestry needle
- 12 inches ⅜-inch wooden dowel
- Green acrylic craft paint to match yarn
- Small foam paintbrush
- ½ yard purple netting
- ½-inch dark green button
- 6 inches silver elastic cord
- Hand-sewing needle
- Purple sewing thread
- Hot-glue gun

Project Note

Use #16 tapestry needle for all stitching. Use #20 tapestry needle for sewing button to front piece.

Critter Catcher

1. Paint dowel with foam brush and green paint, using as many coats as necessary for even, complete coverage; allow to dry thoroughly between coats.
2. Cut two critter catcher pieces from radial circles (page 79), cutting away yellow area.
3. Stitch around circles, using two stitches per hole in the inside row of holes as necessary to cover canvas. Using bright purple, Overcast inside edges and outside edges between arrows.
4. Cut an 18-inch circle from purple netting. Using hand-sewing needle and purple sewing thread, sew a Running Stitch close to edge all around, gathering slightly while sewing. Pull thread to gather net until opening fits around inside edge of circle; knot ends and clip.
5. Glue gathered edge of netting to wrong side of one circle along inside edge. Glue dowel to wrong side of one circle between arrows where outside edge is Overcast.
6. Place wrong sides of circles together, making sure Overcast areas and holes along outside edges are aligned. Whipstitch together along outside edges with bright purple. Glue along inside edges.

Corral Cutting & Stitching

1. Cut corral top, bottom, front, back, side and handle pieces from bright purple plastic canvas according to graphs (pages 78 and 79). Corral bottom will remain unstitched.
2. From clear stiff plastic canvas, cut one 43-hole x 27-hole piece for inner box bottom, two 27-hole x 31-hole pieces for inner box short sides, and two 43-hole x 31-hole pieces for inner box long sides. Inner box pieces will remain unstitched.
3. Stitch corral pieces following graphs, working large fern Cross Stitches and Continental Stitches for lettering first. Using bright purple, work Upright Cross Stitches over Fern Cross Stitches.
4. Stitch dragonflies, working iridescent white Straight Stitches for wings before working center stitches over wings. Work green metallic craft cord French Knots for eyes on top piece.

Corral Assembly

1. Using fern, Whipstitch handle ends to top where indicated with red highlighted lines.
2. Securing tails on backside under stitching for handle, attach silver elastic cord to top with a Lark's Head Knot where indicated on graph, leaving a 1-inch loop for closure. Add a dab of glue to knot.
3. Using 1-ply bright purple, sew button to front over top center Cross Stitch. Knot and fasten securely on wrong side.

4. Using bright purple through step 5, Whipstitch corral sides to top and bottom, then Whipstitch back to top, bottom and sides. Whipstitch front to bottom, leaving side and top edges free. Overcast remaining edge on top. Inside edges on sides will remain unstitched.

5. For inner box, Whipstitch short sides to long sides, then Whipstitch sides to bottom. Top edges will remain unstitched.

6. Slide inner box into critter corral; fasten with button and loop closure. ●

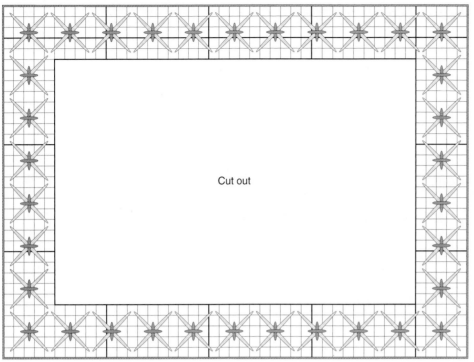

Critter Corral Side
45 holes x 33 holes
Cut 2 from purple

Critter Corral Handle
45 holes x 5 holes
Cut 1 from purple

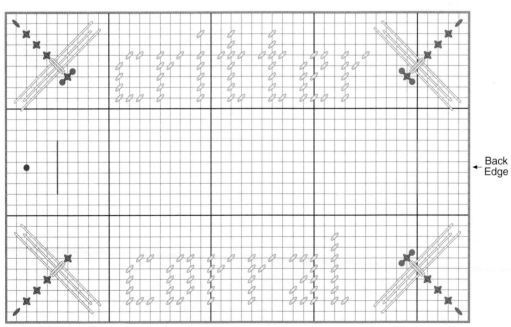

← Back Edge

Critter Corral Top & Bottom
45 holes x 29 holes
Cut 2 from purple
Stitch top as graphed
Do not stitch bottom

COLOR KEY

Plastic Canvas Yarn	Yards
☐ Fern #23	23
■ Bright purple #64	20

Metallic Craft Cord

■ Green #55004	3
● Green #55004 French Knot	

Iridescent Craft Cord

⟋ White #55033 Straight Stitch	3

Color numbers given are for Uniek Needloft
plastic canvas yarn, metallic craft cord and
iridescent craft cord.

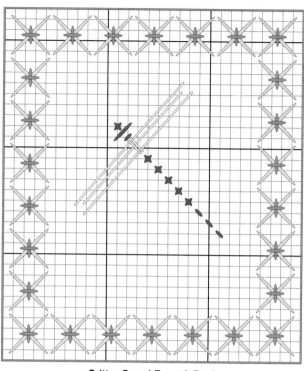

Critter Corral Front & Back
29 holes x 33 holes
Cut 2 from purple

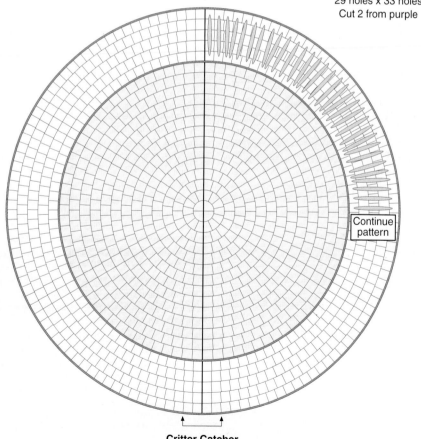

Continue
pattern

Critter Catcher
Cut 2 from radial circles,
cutting away yellow area

Sunflower Garden Coasters

Soak up some sunshine, indoors or out, with these exquisite sunflower coasters!

DESIGNS BY JANELLE GIESE

Skill Level
Intermediate

Size
Coaster: 4³/₈ inches W x 4³/₈ inches H
Holder: 4⁷/₈ inches W x 3¹/₄ inches H x 1³/₄ inches D

Materials
- 1 sheet clear 7-count plastic canvas
- ²/₃ sheet almond Uniek QuickCount 7-count plastic canvas
- Uniek Needloft plastic canvas yarn as listed in color key
- DMC #3 pearl cotton as listed in color key
- DMC #5 pearl cotton: 1 yard white and as listed in color key
- 1 yard DMC 6-strand embroidery floss: pale golden brown #3827
- #16 tapestry needle
- 2 Mill Hill Products bumble bee buttons #86128 from Gay Bowles Sales Inc.
- 2 Mill Hill Products flying bee buttons #86132 from Gay Bowles Sales Inc.

Instructions
1. Cut four coaster backs from almond plastic canvas; cut four coasters, one holder front and one holder back from clear plastic canvas according to graphs. Coaster backs will remain unstitched.

2. From clear plastic canvas, cut two 10-hole x 10-hole pieces for holder sides and one 10-hole x 24-hole piece for holder base.

3. Using moss throughout, Continental Stitch sides and base; Overcast top edges of sides.

4. Stitch remaining pieces following graphs working uncoded areas with baby yellow Continental Stitches and leaving red Whipstitch lines unworked at this time.

5. Using moss and fern Continental Stitches, Whipstitch sides to front and

back along red Whipstitch lines following graph. Whipstitch base to front, back and sides. Overcast all remaining edges.

6. Using ultra dark coffee brown #5 pearl cotton, work Backstitches and Straight Stitches on holder front and back. Using pale golden brown embroidery floss, sew buttons to front and back where indicated on graph.

7. Work light brown #3 pearl cotton Backstitches on coasters over completed background stitching. For each coaster, using yellow, Whipstitch one unworked almond coaster to one stitched coaster.

8. Place coasters in holder so that two coasters are facing front and two facing back. ●

Sunflower Garden Coaster
28 holes x 28 holes
Cut 4 from clear
Stitch as graphed
Cut 4 from almond
Do not stitch

COLOR KEY

Plastic Canvas Yarn	Yards
Maple #13	7
Cinnamon #15	11
Fern #23	2
Moss #25	12
Beige #40	6
Yellow #57	22
Uncoded areas are baby yellow #21 Continental Stitches	15
#3 Pearl Cotton	
✎ Light brown #434 Backstitch	8
#5 Pearl Cotton	
✎ Ultra dark coffee brown #434 Backstitch and Straight Stitch	3
● Attach bumble bee	
● Attach flying bee	

Color numbers given are for Uniek Needloft plastic canvas yarn and DMC #3 and #5 pearl cotton.

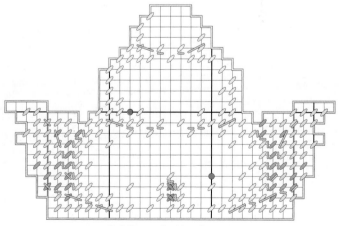

Sunflower Garden Coaster
Holder Front & Back
32 holes x 20 holes
Cut 2 from clear

Bug Fun Bookmarks

These chipper chums will give you several "legs up" on your summer reading!

DESIGNS BY JANNA BRITTON

Skill Level
Beginner

Size
Bee: 1⅝ inches W x 1¼ inches H, excluding ribbon
Ladybug: 1½ inches W x 1½ inches H, excluding ribbon

Materials
Each Bookmark
- Small amount 10-count plastic canvas
- DMC 6-strand embroidery floss as listed in color key
- #18 tapestry needle
- Black extra-fine point permanent marker
- Sewing needle
- Seam sealant (optional)
- Low-temperature glue gun

Bees
- Yellow smiling face Expressions beads #157n and #1591b from The Beadery
- 2 (12-inch) lengths ⅞-inch-wide white grosgrain ribbon
- 2 (15-inch) lengths black mini rickrack
- Black sewing thread
- 9 inches white iridescent chenille stem

Ladybug
- ½-inch black pompom
- 2 (4mm) movable eyes
- 11 inches ⅞-inch-wide white grosgrain ribbon
- 13 inches kelly green mini rickrack
- Kelly green sewing thread

Instructions

1. Cut plastic canvas according to graphs.
2. Stitch and Overcast pieces with 12-ply floss. Work black French Knots on ladybug wings with 6 plies and black Backstitches on ladybug body with 3 plies; using red floss, tack wings to body where indicated by green dots.
3. Use photo as a guide through step 9. For ladybug, glue pompom to front corner of body and movable eyes to pompom, then glue body to top of ribbon.
4. Using sewing needle and kelly green sewing thread, stitch rickrack to ribbon below ladybug in a wavy line. Cut a "V" in ribbon tail. If desired, use seam sealant on ends of ribbon and rickrack to prevent fraying.
5. With black marker, write "fly" and "away" on ribbon, adding dashed lines between words. Write "Home" at the bottom of ribbon if desired.
6. For bees, cut chenille stem in half, then bend each length around two fingers to form wings, twisting ends of each wing together at bottom. Using sewing needle and black sewing thread, stitch one pair of wings to back of each body along top edge.
7. Glue one bead to front of each body where indicated. Glue one bee to top of each ribbon.
8. Using sewing needle and black sewing thread, stitch one length rickrack to each ribbon below bee in a wavy line with some loops. Cut a "V" in ribbon tails. If desired, use seam sealant on ends of ribbon and rickrack to prevent fraying.
9. With black marker, write "Bee" and "cool" on ribbon of bee with sunglasses, adding dashed lines between words. Repeat with remaining ribbon, writing the words "Bee" and "happy." ●

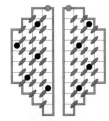

← Front corner

Bookmark Ladybug Body
8 holes x 8 holes
Cut 1

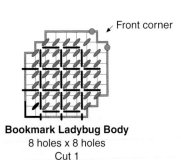

Bookmark Ladybug Wings
4 holes x 10 holes each
Cut 1 each

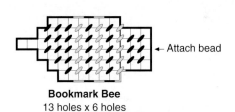

← Attach bead

Bookmark Bee
13 holes x 6 holes
Cut 2

COLOR KEY	
6-Strand Embroidery Floss	**Yards**
■ Black #310	6
■ Bright red #666	3
□ Light topaz #726	2
╱ Red #321 Overcasting	2
╱ Black #310 (3-ply) Backstitch	
● Black #310 (6-ply) French Knot	
Color numbers given are for DMC 6-strand embroidery floss.	

Flights of Fancy

Deliciously diverse like their real-world counterparts, these butterfly designs make you want to stitch every one!

DESIGNS BY KATHLEEN HURLEY

Project Note

The triangle, heart, square, inverted triangle and diamond shapes designate Continental Stitches.

Instructions

1. Cut plastic canvas according to graphs (this page and pages 86 and 87).

2. Stitch pieces following graphs, working Continental Stitches in uncoded areas as follows: butterflies 1, 3, 4, 5 and 9 with black; butterflies 2 and 10 with warm brown; butterflies 6 and 7 with yellow; and butterfly 8 with mid brown.

3. Overcast butterflies as follows: 1 with black; 2 with mid brown; 3 with black, teal and mist green; 4 with black; 5 with black and paddy green; 6 with bronze; 7 with coffee; 8 with mid brown; 9 with black, lavender and blue jewel; 10 with coffee, warm brown and orange.

4. When background stitching and Overcasting are completed, work black pearl cotton embroidery on butterfly 1; work brown pearl cotton embroidery on butterflies 6 and 10.

5. Glue two magnet strips to wrong side of each butterfly. ●

Skill Level

Beginner

Size

From 4½–5⅝ inches W x 2¾ inches H to 3¾ inches H

Materials

- 1½ sheets 7-count plastic canvas
- Coats & Clark Red Heart Classic worsted weight yarn Art. E267 as listed in color key
- #3 pearl cotton as listed in color key
- #16 tapestry needle
- 20 (1-inch) lengths ½-inch-wide magnet strip
- Hot-glue gun

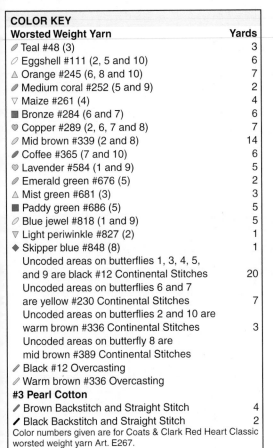

COLOR KEY	
Worsted Weight Yarn	**Yards**
⬤ Teal #48 (3)	3
⬤ Eggshell #111 (2, 5 and 10)	6
△ Orange #245 (6, 8 and 10)	7
⬤ Medium coral #252 (5 and 9)	2
▽ Maize #261 (4)	4
■ Bronze #284 (6 and 7)	6
♡ Copper #289 (2, 6, 7 and 8)	7
⬤ Mid brown #339 (2 and 8)	14
⬤ Coffee #365 (7 and 10)	6
♡ Lavender #584 (1 and 9)	5
⬤ Emerald green #676 (5)	2
△ Mist green #681 (3)	3
■ Paddy green #686 (5)	5
⬤ Blue jewel #818 (1 and 9)	5
▽ Light periwinkle #827 (2)	1
◆ Skipper blue #848 (8)	1
Uncoded areas on butterflies 1, 3, 4, 5, and 9 are black #12 Continental Stitches	20
Uncoded areas on butterflies 6 and 7 are yellow #230 Continental Stitches	7
Uncoded areas on butterflies 2 and 10 are warm brown #336 Continental Stitches	3
Uncoded areas on butterfly 8 are mid brown #389 Continental Stitches	
⬤ Black #12 Overcasting	
⬤ Warm brown #336 Overcasting	
#3 Pearl Cotton	
⬤ Brown Backstitch and Straight Stitch	4
⬤ Black Backstitch and Straight Stitch	2
Color numbers given are for Coats & Clark Red Heart Classic worsted weight yarn Art. E267.	

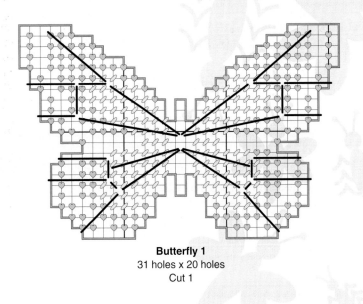

Butterfly 1
31 holes x 20 holes
Cut 1

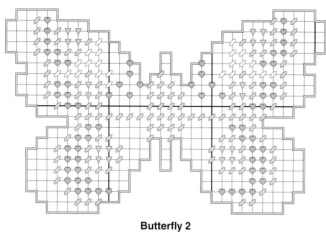

Butterfly 2
31 holes x 19 holes
Cut 1

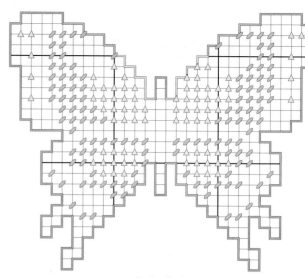

Butterfly 3
29 holes x 24 holes
Cut 1

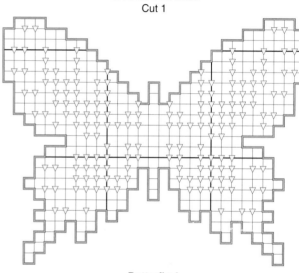

Butterfly 4
29 holes x 23 holes
Cut 1

COLOR KEY

Worsted Weight Yarn	Yards
Teal #48 (3)	3
Eggshell #111 (2, 5 and 10)	6
Orange #245 (6, 8 and 10)	7
Medium coral #252 (5 and 9)	2
Maize #261 (4)	4
Bronze #284 (6 and 7)	6
Copper #289 (2, 6, 7 and 8)	7
Mid brown #339 (2 and 8)	14
Coffee #365 (7 and 10)	6
Lavender #584 (1 and 9)	5
Emerald green #676 (5)	2
Mist green #681 (3)	3
Paddy green #686 (5)	5
Blue jewel #818 (1 and 9)	5
Light periwinkle #827 (2)	1
Skipper blue #848 (8)	1
Uncoded areas on butterflies 1, 3, 4, 5, and 9 are black #12 Continental Stitches	20
Uncoded areas on butterflies 6 and 7 are yellow #230 Continental Stitches	7
Uncoded areas on butterflies 2 and 10 are warm brown #336 Continental Stitches	3
Uncoded areas on butterfly 8 are mid brown #389 Continental Stitches	
Black #12 Overcasting	
Warm brown #336 Overcasting	
#3 Pearl Cotton	
Brown Backstitch and Straight Stitch	4
Black Backstitch and Straight Stitch	2

Color numbers given are for Coats & Clark Red Heart Classic worsted weight yarn Art. E267.

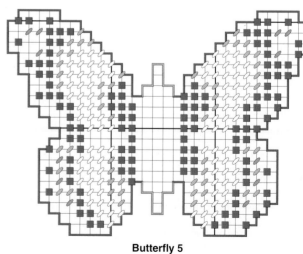

Butterfly 5
29 holes x 21 holes
Cut 1

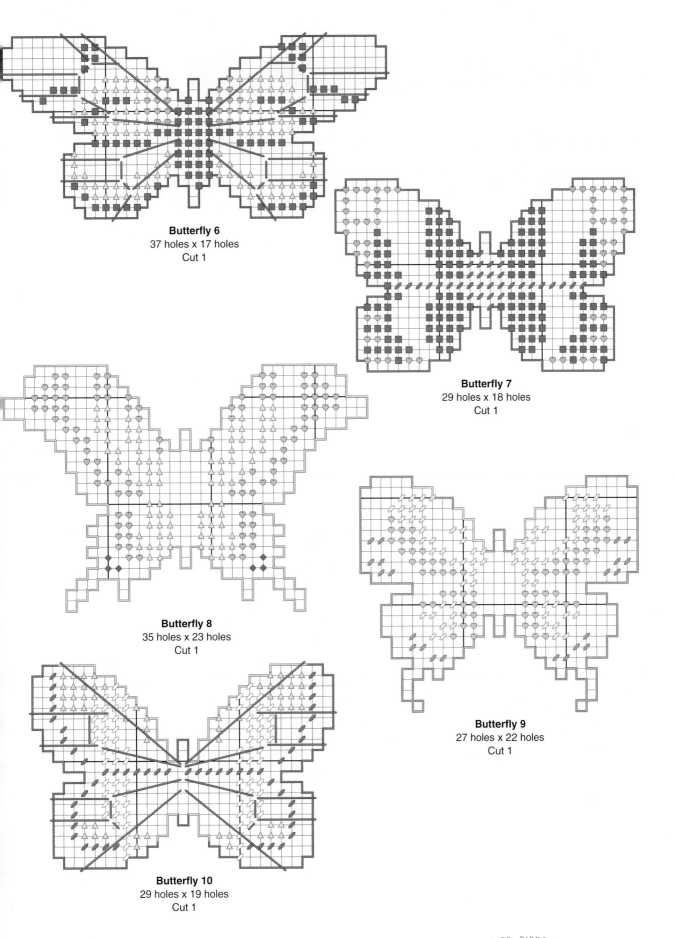

Butterfly 6
37 holes x 17 holes
Cut 1

Butterfly 7
29 holes x 18 holes
Cut 1

Butterfly 8
35 holes x 23 holes
Cut 1

Butterfly 9
27 holes x 22 holes
Cut 1

Butterfly 10
29 holes x 19 holes
Cut 1

Summer Calendar

Keep track of those hot summer dates with this sun-speckled calendar!

DESIGN BY ANGIE ARICKX

Skill Level
Beginner

Size
13½ inches W x 11 inches H;
fits calendar sheet 11 inches W x
8½ inches H

Materials
- 3 sheets 7-count plastic canvas
- Uniek Needloft plastic canvas yarn as listed in color key
- #16 tapestry needle
- Sawtooth hanger
- Hot-glue gun

Project Note
Some graphs are shared with similar calendars in other chapters of this book. Colors used for each season are given with the graphs and/or the instructions for that season.

Instructions
1. Following graphs throughout, cut sunflower, girl and boy; cut frame, spacer, leaves and fence (pages 22, 24 and 25). Cut one 81-hole x 65-hole piece for calendar frame back.

2. Stitch and Overcast fence with white and leaves with holly. Stitch and Overcast girl, boy and sunflowers following graphs, working French Knots on sunflowers last.

3. Using fern through step 4, stitch calendar frame front, leaving area shaded with yellow unworked for now. Overcast inside and outside edges.

4. Center spacer, then frame back over unworked area on wrong side of calendar front. ***Note:*** *Spacer should be between frame front and back.* Complete pattern stitch on frame front in shaded yellow area, working through all three layers.

5. Using photo as a guide, glue fence, sunflowers and leaves to frame front; glue girl to bottom left corner and boy to bottom right corner. Glue hanger to frame back. Insert calendar through opening on right side. ●

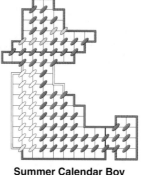

Summer Calendar Boy
13 holes x 15 holes
Cut 1

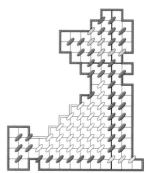

Summer Calendar Girl
13 holes x 15 holes
Cut 1

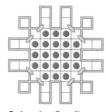

Calendar Sunflower
9 holes x 9 holes
Cut 12

COLOR KEY	
Plastic Canvas Yarn	**Yards**
■ Red #01	1
■ Cinnamon #14	14
Fern #23	40
Holly #27	5
■ Royal #32	2
□ White #41	10
□ Flesh tone #56	1
□ Yellow #57	12
● Cinnamon #14 French Knot	
Color numbers given are for Uniek Needloft plastic canvas yarn.	

Night Light Bug

With its friendly smile and cheerful colors, this night light buddy keeps the bogeyman from "bugging" you!

DESIGN BY LAURA VICTORY

Skill Level
Beginner

Size
7¼ inches W x 8¼ inches H

Materials
- ½ sheet 7-count plastic canvas
- Uniek Needloft plastic canvas yarn as listed in color key
- 6-strand embroidery floss as listed in color key
- #16 tapestry needle
- 2 (15mm) movable eyes
- 12 inches red chenille stem
- 2 (½-inch) purple iridescent pompoms
- Indiglo night light
- Hot-glue gun

Instructions
1. Cut plastic according to graphs. Cut red chenille stem in half.

2. Stitch and Overcast pieces following graphs. When background stitching is completed, work red Backstitches for mouth; outline red and bright orange hearts with 2-ply black floss.

3. Using photo as a guide through step 5, attach feet to body with purple yarn. Glue eyes to head and head to body.

4. For antennae, wrap chenille stems around pencil to coil, then thread stems from front to back through holes at top of head. Glue antennae to back of head; glue pompoms to top of antennae.

5. Glue night light to bug, allowing light to show through opening on body. ●

COLOR KEY

Plastic Canvas Yarn	Yards
■ Red #01	2
▨ Purple #46	4
☐ Yellow #57	24
▨ Bright orange #58	2
╱ Red #01 Backstitch	

6-Strand Embroidery Floss

╱ Black (2-ply) Backstitch	1

Color numbers given are for Uniek Needloft plastic canvas yarn.

Night Light Bug Foot
7 holes x 6 holes
Cut 3

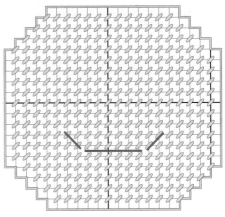

Night Light Bug Head
21 holes x 19 holes
Cut 1

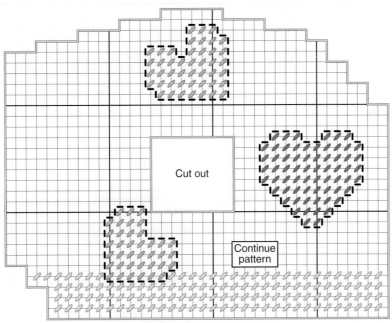

Night Light Bug Body
37 holes x 29 holes
Cut 1

Bumbly Bee Napkin Ring

This honey of a holder keeps your table "abuzz" with happy smiles!

DESIGN BY JUDY COLLISHAW

Skill Level

Beginner

Size

4³⁄₈ inches W x 5¼ inches H x 2³⁄₈ inches D

Materials

- ½ sheet 7-count plastic canvas
- Worsted weight yarn as listed in color key
- #5 pearl cotton as listed in color key
- #16 tapestry needle
- 6 inches ⅛-inch-wide pale blue double-sided satin ribbon
- Hot-glue gun

Instructions

1. Cut plastic canvas according to graphs.
2. Stitch and Overcast feet and head pieces following graphs, working black Backstitches on head while stitching.
3. When background stitching is completed, Backstitch red pearl cotton mouth and work black yarn French Knots on head.
4. Stitch body following graph. Fold body in half with wrong sides together and Whipstitch 7-hole edges together; Overcast all remaining edges.
5. Glue center of feet to body bottom. Glue head at a slight angle to top of body front. Tie ribbon in a small bow and glue to body under chin. ●

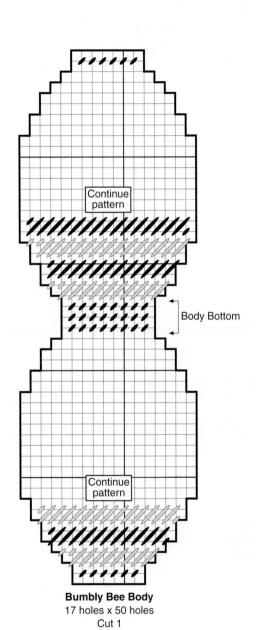

Bumbly Bee Body
17 holes x 50 holes
Cut 1

Continue
pattern

Continue
pattern

Body Bottom

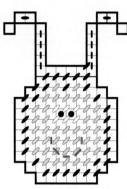

Bumbly Bee Head
12 holes x 16 holes
Cut 1

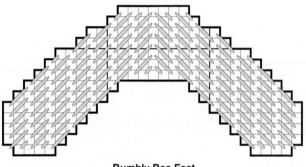

Bumbly Bee Feet
29 holes x 14 holes
Cut 1

COLOR KEY	
Worsted Weight Yarn	**Yards**
■ Black	10
▨ Bright yellow	7
▨ Rose	1
☐ White	1
╱ Black Backstitch	
● Black French Knot	
#5 Pearl Cotton	
╱ Red Backstitch	1

Honey-Do List

Here's a warmhearted way to accomplish those chores—stitch a playful reminder that everyone will enjoy!

DESIGN BY SUSAN LEINBERGER

Project Note

Use #16 tapestry needle with yarn and #20 tapestry needle with pearl cotton.

Painting, Cutting & Stitching

1. Paint chalkboard frame with white acrylic paint; allow to dry.

2. Cut header, bear, arm, chalk tray pieces, leaves, flowers and beehive from 7-count plastic canvas; cut bees from 10-count plastic canvas according to graphs (pages 96 and 97). Cut one 27-hole x 4-hole piece for chalk tray base from 7-count plastic canvas.

3. Stitch and Overcast flowers, working two with purple as graphed and three each replacing purple with red and Christmas red.

4. Continental Stitch chalk tray base with fern. Stitch remaining chalk tray pieces following graphs, reversing one side before stitching. Work holly Backstitches and Straight Stitches on back when background stitching is completed.

5. Using holly throughout and with wrong sides facing, Whipstitch chalk tray front to sides; Whipstitch back to sides with back piece facing front. Whipstitch front, back and sides to base; Overcast remaining edges.

6. Stitch and Overcast remaining pieces following graphs, working uncoded background on header with yellow yarn Continental Stitches and leaving wings on bees unstitched as shown.

7. When background stitching is completed, work embroidery on bear and header with pearl cotton. Work yellow yarn French Knots on flowers and holly yarn Straight Stitches on leaves.

Assembly

1. Cut six varying lengths of 34-gauge wire. Wrap wire around toothpick to make coils. Insert one end of wire coils into stitching on back of bees, leaving one half bee without a coil; secure with a dab of glue.

2. Use photo as a guide throughout assembly. For eye, glue 6mm cabochon to head of bear where indicated on graph. Glue half bee without wire coil to top edge of bear paw; glue bear arm to bear, and flowers to leaves and chalk tray back.

3. Attach full bees to bear's nose and head, and half bees to hive, leaves and chalk tray by inserting end of wire coils into stitching and securing with a dab of tacky glue.

4. Attach sawtooth hanger to top center back of chalkboard.

5. Using hot glue, attach header, bear, chalk tray, leaves and beehive to chalkboard frame. ●

Skill Level

Intermediate

Size

10¾ inches W x 12¼ inches H

Materials

- 1 sheet 7-count plastic canvas
- Small amount 10-count plastic canvas
- Uniek Needloft plastic canvas yarn as listed in color key
- Coats & Clark Anchor #3 pearl cotton as listed in color key
- #16 tapestry needle
- #20 tapestry needle
- 7-inch x 10-inch chalkboard with wooden frame
- White acrylic craft paint
- Small foam paintbrush
- 6mm round black cabochon
- 34-gauge beading wire
- Round toothpick
- Chalk
- Saw-tooth hanger
- Tacky craft glue
- Hot-glue gun

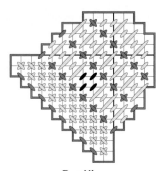

Bee Hive
14 holes x 14 holes
Cut 1 from 7-count

Half Bee
7 holes x 7 holes
Cut 5 from 10-count

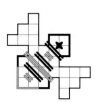

Full Bee
8 holes x 8 holes
Cut 2 from 10-count

Flower
6 holes x 6 holes
Cut 8 from 7-count
Stitch 2 as graphed
Stitch 3 each replacing purple
with red and Christmas red

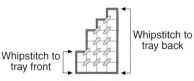

Whipstitch to
tray front

Whipstitch to
tray back

Chalk Tray Side
4 holes x 6 holes
Cut 2 from 7-count, reverse 1

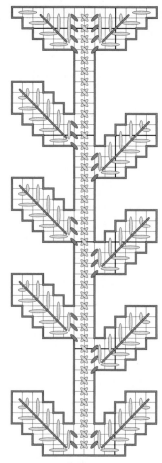

Leaves
14 holes x 42 holes
Cut 1 from 7-count

Chalk Tray Front
27 holes x 2 holes
Cut 1 from 7-count

Chalk Tray Back
27 holes x 8 holes
Cut 1 from 7-count

COLOR KEY

Plastic Canvas Yarn	Yards
▨ Black #00	2
Red #01	3
Christmas red #02	3
▨ Maple #13	5
▨ Cinnamon #14	15
▨ Fern #23	7
▨ Holly #27	7
▨ Beige #40	5
▨ Purple #46	2
▨ Yellow #57	12

Uncoded areas are yellow
#57 Continental Stitches

✦ Holly #27 Backstitch
and Straight Stitch

○ Yellow #57 French Knot

#3 Pearl Cotton

■ Black #403	5
✦ Light topaz #305 Straight Stitch	3
✦ Very dark topaz #310 Backstitch	3

✦ Black #403 Backstitch
and Straight Stitch

● Black #403 French Knot

○ Attach cabochon

Color numbers given are for Uniek Needloft
plastic canvas yarn and Coats & Clark Anchor
#3 pearl cotton.

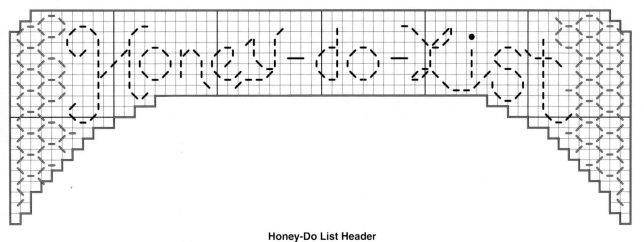

Honey-Do List Header
60 holes x 20 holes
Cut 1 from 7-count

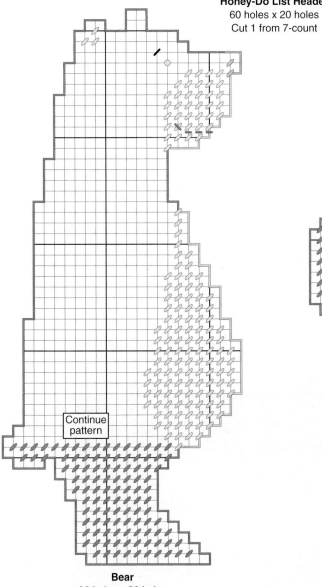

Bear
23 holes x 52 holes
Cut 1 from 10-count

Continue pattern

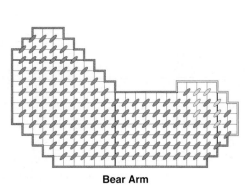

Bear Arm
22 holes x 13 holes
Cut 1 from 7-count

Vintage Rose Tissue Topper

Whisk yourself back to the moonlit gardens of summers past with this vibrant vintage rose!

DESIGN BY JANELLE GIESE

Skill Level
Advanced

Size
Fits boutique-style tissue box

Materials
- 1½ sheets black 7-count plastic canvas
- Coats & Clark Red Heart Classic worsted weight yarn Art. E267 as listed in color key
- Coats & Clark Red Heart Super Saver worsted weight yarn Art. E300 as listed in color key
- Kreinik Medium (#16) Braid as listed in color key
- Kreinik Cord as listed in color key
- #3 pearl cotton as listed in color key
- #16 tapestry needle
- Thick white glue

Instructions

1. Cut plastic canvas according to graphs.
2. Stitch pieces following graphs, working uncoded areas with black Continental Stitches and using 2 strands when working Cross Stitches with heliodor braid.
3. When background stitching is completed, work black pearl cotton embroidery; use 1-ply medium sage to Straight Stitch stem of leaf.
4. Work heliodor Backstitches and Straight Stitches. To outline rose on front, use 1-strand heliodor braid for laid thread and 1-strand gold cord for couching thread. For circle on top, use 2-strand heliodor braid for laid thread and 1-strand cord for couching thread.
5. Using black yarn throughout, Overcast inside edges of top and bottom edges of front, back and sides. Whipstitch front and back to sides, then Whipstitch front, back and sides to top. ●

COLOR KEY

Worsted Weight Yarn	Yards
☐ Black #12	67
☐ Teal #48	1
☐ Light sage #631	1
■ Medium sage #632	1
☐ Lily pink #719	10
☐ Pale rose #755	10
☐ Cameo rose #759	9
■ Claret #762	7

Uncoded areas are black
#12 Continental Stitches

Medium (#16) Braid

☐ Heliodor #3221	14
╱ Heliodor #3221 Backstitch, Straight Stitch and Laid Couching Stitch	

Cord

╱ Gold #002C Couching Stitch	4

#3 Pearl Cotton

╱ Black Backstitch and Straight Stitch	1

Color numbers given are for Coats & Clark Red Heart Classic worsted weight yarn Art. E267 and Super Saver worsted weight yarn Art. E300 and Kreinik Medium (#16) Braid and Cord.

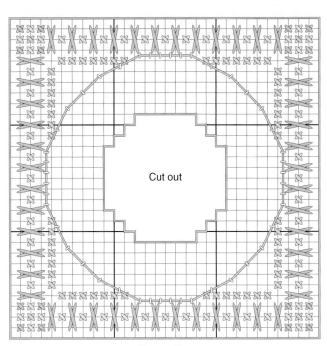

Topper Top
30 holes x 30 holes
Cut 1

Cut out

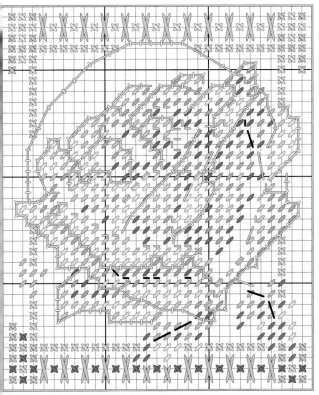

Topper Front
30 holes x 36 holes
Cut 1

Topper Side & Back
30 holes x 36 holes
Cut 3

Blossom Doily & Napkin Ring

This exquisite set has the polished precision of fine stained glass and the perfect beauty of nature's finest flowers!

DESIGNS BY KATHY WIRTH

Skill Level
Intermediate

Size
Doily: 11½ inches W x 11½ inches L
Napkin Ring: 6 inches W x 4¾ inches H

Materials
- 5 Uniek QuickShape plastic canvas hearts
- Small amount black 7-count plastic canvas
- Uniek Needloft plastic canvas yarn as listed in color key
- #16 tapestry needle
- Hot-glue gun
- Thick white glue

Instructions

1. Cut four motifs for doily and one motif for napkin ring from plastic canvas heart shapes according to graphs, cutting away gray areas. Cut one 36-hole x 6-hole piece from black plastic canvas for napkin ring. Napkin ring will remain unstitched.

2. Stitch motifs following graphs; Overcast with black.

3. Position doily motifs with straight edges together and points in center. Using black yarn, tack pieces together at blue dots.

4. Roll napkin ring in a circle, overlapping three holes. Using black, Whipstitch together along short edges of overlap.

5. Glue seams of napkin ring to center back of napkin ring motif. ●

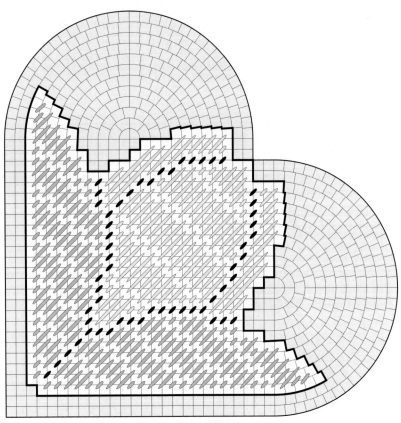

Blossom Napkin Ring Motif
Cut 1 from plastic canvas heart,
cutting away gray areas

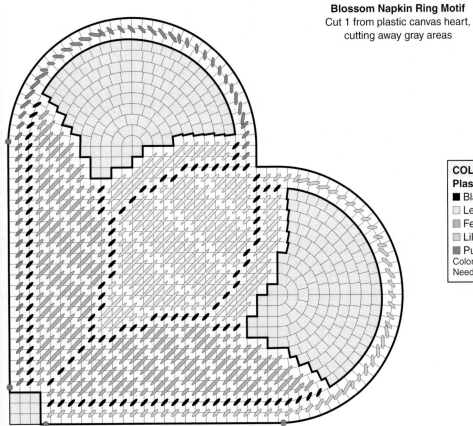

Blossom Doily Motif
Cut 4 from plastic canvas hearts,
cutting away gray areas

COLOR KEY

Plastic Canvas Yarn	Yards
■ Black #00	28
☐ Lemon #20	15
▨ Fern #23	22
▨ Lilac #45	5
▨ Purple #46	8

Color numbers given are for Uniek
Needloft plastic canvas yarn.

Autumn

Autumn is here and is filled with the sights and the sounds of the season! From falling leaves to bugs on the breeze, our exciting assortment of fall projects helps you celebrate in splendid style!

Autumn Bugs

Fluttering in the hay and rustling like the leaves, this butterfly and bee will spice up your spirit!

DESIGNS BY PAM BULL

Instructions

1. Cut plastic canvas according to graphs (this page and page 104).

2. Stitch pieces following graphs. Overcast bee body with black, bee wings with ultra very light tan, butterfly body with black and light tan, and butterfly wings with medium orange spice, ecru and terra cotta.

3. When background stitching and Overcasting are completed, work Backstitches and Straight Stitches with 2-ply black.

4. For butterfly arrangement, tie several strands raffia in a 5-inch-wide bow, leaving long tails. Glue butterfly wings to tails approximately 4 inches from bow.

5. Glue three leaves to back of knot on bow. Cut a 6-inch length of raffia and glue ends to center back of leaves, forming a loop for hanging.

6. For bee arrangement, use twice as much raffia as for butterfly, then tie in a 7-inch-wide bow.

7. Glue four autumn leaves together behind bee, then glue bee and leaf arrangement to front of bow.

8. Glue eyes to tops of heads. ●

Skill Level

Beginner

Size

Bee: 3³⁄₈ inches W x 2¼ inches H, excluding raffia bow

Butterfly: 5½ inches W x 3⁵⁄₈ inches H, excluding raffia bow

Materials

- ½ sheet 10-count plastic canvas
- DMC 6-strand embroidery floss as listed in color key
- #18 tapestry needle
- 4 (7mm) movable eyes
- 1-yard-long strands raffia
- 7 autumn silk leaves
- Hot-glue gun

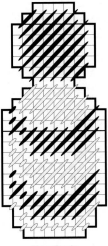

Bee Body
10 holes x 22 holes
Cut 1

COLOR KEY	
6-Strand Embroidery Floss	**Yards**
☐ Ecru	8
■ Black #310	6
▨ Light tan #437	4
▨ Medium orange spice #721	5
☐ Light orange spice #722	3
☐ Ultra very light tan #739	8
▨ Light tangerine #742	1
☐ Medium topaz #783	2
▨ Very dark terra cotta #3777	2
☐ Terra cotta #3830	4
╱ Black #310 Backstitch and Straight Stitch	
Color numbers given are for DMC 6-strand embroidery floss.	

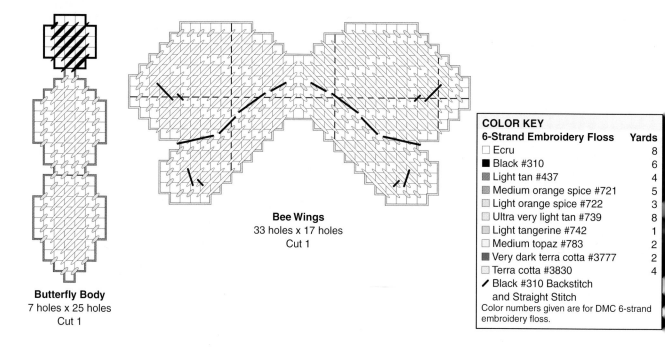

Bee Wings
33 holes x 17 holes
Cut 1

Butterfly Body
7 holes x 25 holes
Cut 1

COLOR KEY

6-Strand Embroidery Floss	Yards
☐ Ecru	8
■ Black #310	6
▨ Light tan #437	4
▨ Medium orange spice #721	5
☐ Light orange spice #722	3
☐ Ultra very light tan #739	8
▨ Light tangerine #742	1
☐ Medium topaz #783	2
■ Very dark terra cotta #3777	2
☐ Terra cotta #3830	4
✎ Black #310 Backstitch and Straight Stitch	

Color numbers given are for DMC 6-strand embroidery floss.

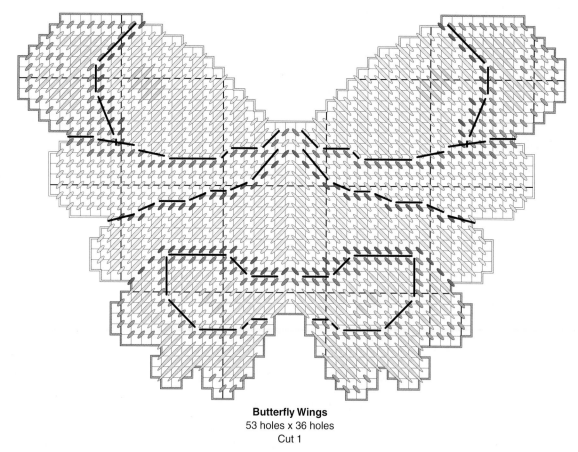

Butterfly Wings
53 holes x 36 holes
Cut 1

Butterfly Bookmark

With a flash and a flutter, this brilliant butterfly marks your resting place!

DESIGN BY SUE PENROD

Skill Level
Beginner

Size
3½ inches W x 3⅛ inches H

Materials
- Small amount 7-count plastic canvas
- Worsted weight yarn as listed in color key
- 6-strand embroidery floss as listed in color key
- #16 tapestry needle
- Small amount black felt
- Large paper clip
- Hot-glue gun

Instructions
1. Cut butterfly from plastic canvas according to graph. Cut felt slightly smaller all around than butterfly.
2. Stitch and Overcast piece following graph, working uncoded background with orange Continental Stitches.
3. Using 3-ply floss, work black Backstitches and white French Knots.
4. Glue felt to wrong side of butterfly, then glue large loop of paper clip over felt to back of body. ●

Butterfly Bookmark
25 holes x 25 holes
Cut 1

COLOR KEY	
Worsted Weight Yarn	**Yards**
■ Black	2
Uncoded background is orange Continental Stitches	2
6-Strand Embroidery Floss	
✎ Black (3-ply) Backstitch	1
○ White (3-ply) French Knot	1

Bittersweet & Blossoms

Celebrate the vibrant hues of autumn with the spicy glow of these beautiful blooms!

DESIGN BY MARY T. COSGROVE

Skill Level
Intermediate

Size
Fits boutique-style tissue box

Materials
- 1½ sheets 7-count plastic canvas
- ¼ sheet 10-count plastic canvas
- Uniek Needloft plastic canvas as listed in color key
- DMC 6-strand embroidery floss as listed in color key
- Kreinik ⅛-inch metallic ribbon as listed in color key
- Bucilla 4mm silk ribbon from Plaid as listed in color key
- #16 tapestry needle
- #18 tapestry needle
- 8 (6-inch) lengths lilac craft wire
- ⅛-inch dowel

Instructions

1. Cut topper sides and top from 7-count plastic canvas; cut flowers and flower centers from 10-count plastic canvas according to graphs.

2. Stitch topper pieces with yarn following graphs, filling in uncoded areas with beige Continental Stitches last. Overcast bottom edges of sides and inside edges of top with beige.

3. When background stitching and Overcasting are completed, work copper braid Straight Stitches and purple Backstitches.

4. Stitch and Overcast flowers and flower centers with 6-ply floss, but do not work Cross Stitch in middle of flower centers.

5. Using lilac silk ribbon, work 12 Turkey Loop Stitches for each of flower's petals where indicated on graph.

6. Using very dark violet floss throughout, tack one flower center over center of each flower with a Cross Stitch. Place flowers in center of Turkey Loop Stitches and tack edges to sides.

7. On each side, thread ends of one wire from back to front through two left holes at top of vase. Repeat with second wire, threading through two holes on right side at top of vase. Wind ends of wire around dowel to form curls.

8. Using beige, Whipstitch sides together, then Whipstitch sides to top. ●

**Bittersweet & Blossoms
Flower Center**
6 holes x 6 holes
Cut 8 from 10-count
Stitch with embroidery floss

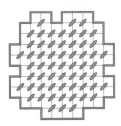

Bittersweet & Blossoms Flower
10 holes x 10 holes
Cut 8 from 10-count
Stitch with embroidery floss

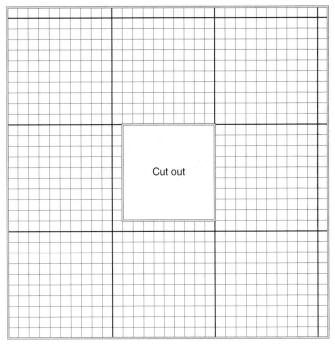

Cut out

Bittersweet & Blossoms Top
31 holes x 31 holes
Cut 1 from 7-count
Stitch with yarn

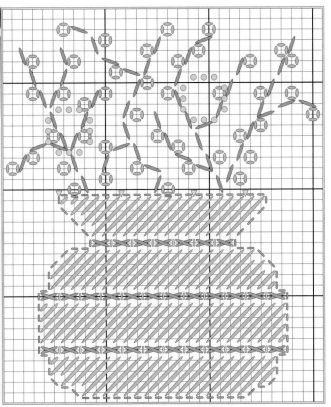

Bittersweet & Blossoms Side
31 holes x 37 holes
Cut 4 from 7-count
Stitch with yarn and ribbon

COLOR KEY	
Plastic Canvas Yarn	**Yards**
▪ Cinnamon #14	8
▫ Fern #23	18
▪ Purple #46	14
▪ Bittersweet #52	10
Uncoded areas are beige	
#40 Continental Stitches	57
╱ Beige #40 Overcasting	
and Whipstitching	
╱ Purple #46 Backstitch	
6-Strand Embroidery Floss	
▪ Very dark violet #550	12
▫ Dark straw #3820	4
╱ Dark orange spice	
#720 Overcasting	4
¹⁄₈-Inch Metallic Ribbon	
╱ Copper #021 Straight Stitch	3
4mm Silk Ribbon	
● Lilac #009 Turkey	
Loop Stitches	8
▽ Attach wire	
Color numbers given are for Uniek Needloft plastic canvas yarn, DMC 6-strand embroidery floss, Kreinik ¹⁄₈-Inch Ribbon and Bucilla 4mm silk ribbon.	

Autumn Birdhouse Hideaway

Radiant with the colors of sun-baked earth and burning embers, this exquisite birdhouse makes the perfect fall accent!

DESIGN BY ANGIE ARICKX

Skill Level
Beginner

Size
Fits two boutique-style tissue boxes, one family-size tissue box, two bathroom tissue rolls or one roll of paper towels

Materials
- 3½ sheets 7-count plastic canvas
- Uniek Needloft plastic canvas yarn as listed in color key
- #16 tapestry needle
- Hot-glue gun

Instructions

1. Cut plastic canvas according to graphs (this page and pages 110 and 111).

2. Following graphs, stitch and Overcast sunflowers, leaves, windows and bird doors.

3. Stitch remaining pieces following graphs, leaving red Whipstitch lines and area inside these lines unworked.

4. When background stitching is completed, work forest Straight Stitches on fences and tangerine French Knots on windows.

5. Using rust throughout, Whipstitch fence pieces together along side edges between arrows; Overcast all remaining fence edges. For each perch, Whipstitch one front to four sides, then Whipstitch sides together. Whipstitch back edges of perches to peak sides along red lines.

6. Using gold, Overcast bottom edges of roof and roof eaves from dot to dot. Whipstitch top edges of roof pieces together, then Whipstitch eaves to roof sides.

7. Using forest, Whipstitch peak sides to flat sides; Overcast top and bottom edges.

8. Center and glue bird doors over black circles on peak sides; center and glue windows over black squares on all four sides. Place birdhouse inside fence and tack with glue. Glue roof to top of birdhouse.

9. Using photo as a guide, glue sunflowers to top of each Straight Stitch on fences; glue two leaves to bottom of each stem. Glue one sunflower and two leaves under each roof peak. ●

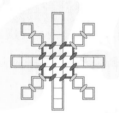

Birdhouse Hideaway Sunflower
9 holes x 9 holes
Cut 10

Birdhouse Hideaway Leaf
4 holes x 4 holes
Cut 20

**Birdhouse Hideaway
Perch Front**
3 holes x 3 holes
Cut 2

**Birdhouse Hideaway
Perch Side**
6 holes x 3 holes
Cut 8

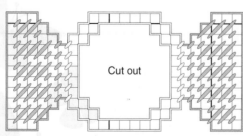

Birdhouse Hideaway Bird Door
23 holes x 11 holes
Cut 2

COLOR KEY	
Plastic Canvas Yarn	**Yards**
■ Black #00	17
■ Rust #09	41
■ Cinnamon #14	4
☐ Gold #17	54
☐ Moss #25	12
■ Forest #29	131
☐ Beige #40	14
☐ Yellow #57	8
╱ Forest #29 Straight Stitch	
● Tangerine #11 French Knot	2
Color numbers given are for Uniek Needloft plastic canvas yarn.	

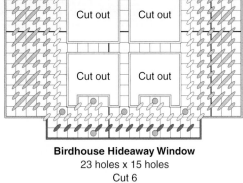

Birdhouse Hideaway Window
23 holes x 15 holes
Cut 6

Birdhouse Hideaway Roof Eaves
29 holes x 29 holes
Cut 2

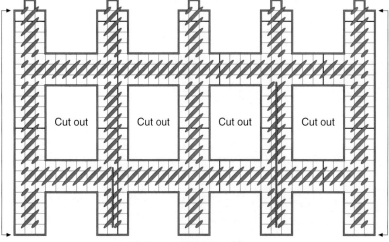

Birdhouse Hideaway Fence
35 holes x 22 holes
Cut 4

COLOR KEY	
Plastic Canvas Yarn	**Yards**
■ Black #00	17
■ Rust #09	41
■ Cinnamon #14	4
■ Gold #17	54
□ Moss #25	12
■ Forest #29	131
□ Beige #40	14
□ Yellow #57	8
╱ Forest #29 Straight Stitch	
● Tangerine #11 French Knot	2
Color numbers given are for Uniek Needloft plastic canvas yarn.	

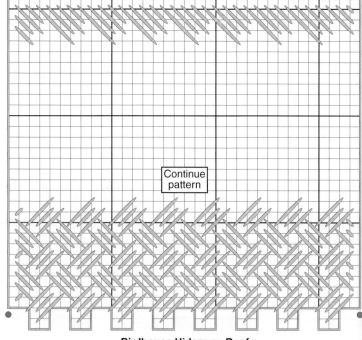

Continue pattern

Birdhouse Hideaway Roof
34 holes x 31 holes
Cut 2

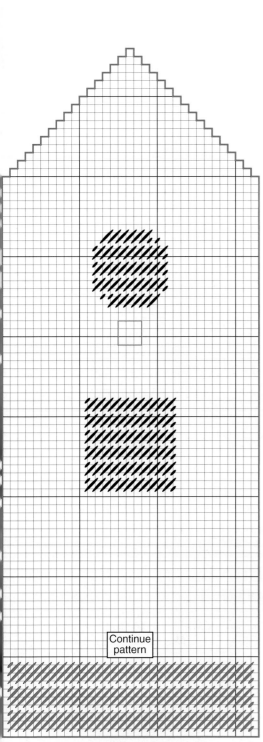

Birdhouse Hideaway Peak Side
33 holes x 86 holes
Cut 2

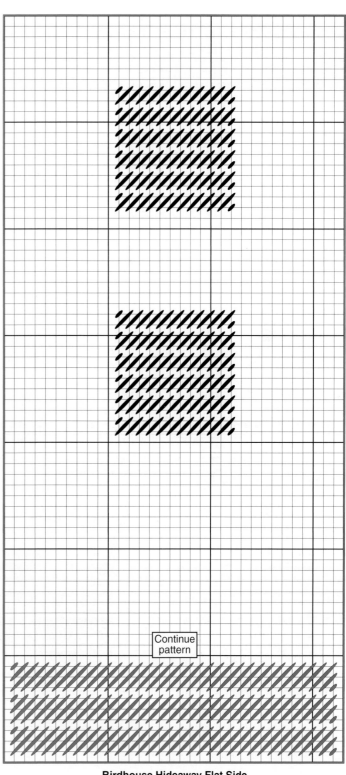

Birdhouse Hideaway Flat Side
33 holes x 70 holes
Cut 2

Centipede Memo Magnets

Leggy and lively, these mischievous mites are more than happy to lend a "hand!"

DESIGNS BY SUSAN LEINBERGER

Skill Level
Beginner

Size
3⅛ inches W x 6¼ inches H, excluding legs and antennae

Materials
- ¼ sheet Uniek QuickCount bright green 7-count plastic canvas
- ¼ sheet Uniek QuickCount bright purple 7-count plastic canvas
- Uniek Needloft plastic canvas yarn as listed in color key
- #3 pearl cotton as listed in color key
- #16 tapestry needle
- 4 (10mm) oval movable eyes
- 7mm yellow pompom
- 7mm orange pompom
- 22-gauge Fun Wire from Toner Plastics:
  24 inches yellow
  24 inches orange
  12 inches purple
  12 inches green
- Nail clipper
- 6 (½-inch) round magnets
- Hot-glue gun

Instructions

1. Cut one centipede each from bright green and bright purple plastic canvas according to graphs.

2. Following graphs throughout, stitch green centipede with fern and yellow; Overcast with holly. Stitch purple centipede with bright purple and orange; Overcast with purple.

3. When background stitching is completed, work black pearl cotton Backstitches for mouth.

4. Using photo as a guide through step 7, for antennae, bend green and purple wires in half and coil each end away from center. Glue green antennae to top backside of green centipede and purple antennae to top backside of purple centipede.

5. For legs, use nail clipper to cut yellow and orange wire in half so there are two 12-inch lengths of both colors.

6. Using yellow wire with green centipede and orange wire with purple centipede, glue center of lengths to wrong sides of centipedes where indicated with arrows. Coil ends toward center.

7. Glue eyes to heads. For noses, glue yellow pompom to green centipede and orange pompom to purple centipede.

8. Glue three magnets to back of each centipede.

9. Insert photos or notes into coils. ●

COLOR KEY	
Plastic Canvas Yarn	**Yards**
☐ Fern #23	4
☐ Yellow #57	2
☐ Bright orange #58	2
☐ Bright purple #64	4
⁄ Holly #27 Overcasting	2
⁄ Purple #46 Overcasting	2
#3 Pearl Cotton	
⁄ Black Backstitch	1
Color numbers given are for Uniek Needloft plastic canvas yarn.	

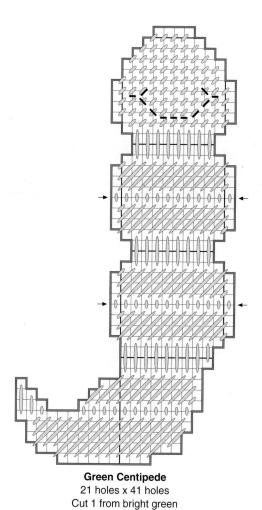

Green Centipede
21 holes x 41 holes
Cut 1 from bright green

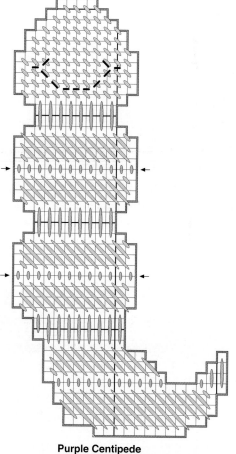

Purple Centipede
21 holes x 41 holes
Cut 1 from bright purple

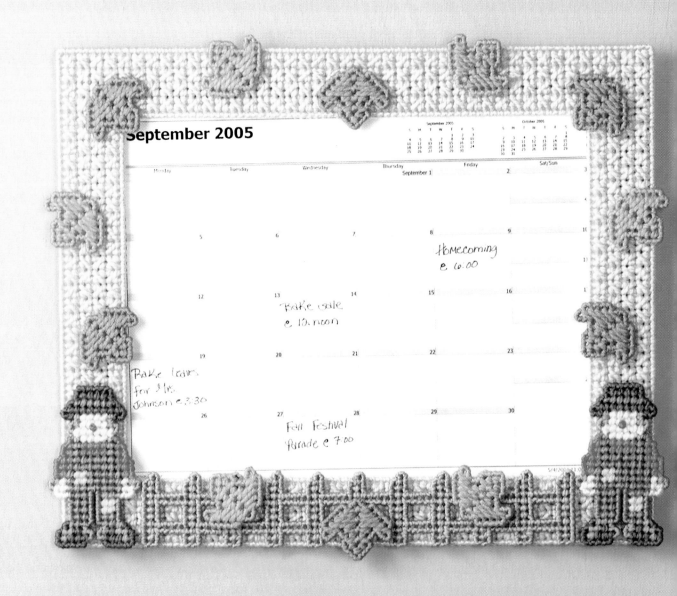

September 2005

| September 2005 | | | | | October 2005 | |

Monday	Tuesday	Wednesday	Thursday	Friday	Sat/Sun
			September 1	2	3
5	6	7	8 Homecoming @ 6:00	9	10 11
12	13 Bake sale @ 12 noon	14	15	16	17 18
19 Bake cakes for Mrs. Johnson @ 3:30	20	21	22	23	24 25
26	27 Fall Festival Parade @ 7:00	28	29	30	

Autumn Calendar

Keep your heart happy with this clever calendar, full of falling leaves and festive fun!

DESIGN BY ANGIE ARICKX

Project Note

Some graphs are shared with similar calendars in other chapters of this book. Colors used for each season are given with the graphs and/or the instructions for that season.

Instructions

1. Following graphs throughout, cut leaves and scarecrows; cut frame, spacer and fence (pages 24 and 25). Cut one 81-hole x 65-hole piece for calendar frame back.

2. Stitch and Overcast fence with camel. Stitch scarecrows and leaves following graphs, working six leaves with rust as graphed and six with pumpkin. Work

Backstitches on leaves and French Knots on scarecrows last.

3. Using beige through step 4, stitch calendar frame front, leaving area shaded with yellow unworked for now. Overcast inside and outside edges.

4. Center spacer, then frame back over unworked area on wrong side of calendar front. **Note:** *Spacer should be between frame front and back.* Complete pattern stitch on frame front in shaded yellow area, working through all three layers.

5. Using photo as a guide, glue fence and leaves to frame front; glue scarecrows to bottom corners. Glue hanger to frame back. Insert calendar through opening on right side. ●

Skill Level

Beginner

Size

13¾ inches W x 11 inches H; fits calendar sheet 11 inches W x 8½ inches H

Materials

- 3 sheets 7-count plastic canvas
- Uniek Needloft plastic canvas yarn as listed in color key
- #16 tapestry needle
- Sawtooth hanger
- Hot-glue gun

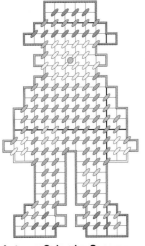

Autumn Calendar Scarecrow
13 holes x 22 holes
Cut 2

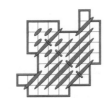

Autumn Calendar Scarecrow
8 holes x 8 holes
Cut 12
Stitch 6 as graphed
Stitch 6 with pumpkin

COLOR KEY	
Plastic Canvas Yarn	**Yards**
■ Rust #09	6
Pumpkin #12	6
■ Cinnamon #14	2
□ Gold #17	2
Beige #40	40
Camel #43	9
■ Bittersweet #52	2
■ Turquoise #54	3
□ Flesh tone #56	2
□ Yellow #57	1
╱ Rust #09 Backstitch	
● Bittersweet #52 French Knot	
Color numbers given are for Uniek Needloft plastic canvas yarn.	

A Touch of Autumn

You'll always enjoy the brisk autumn breeze when you hang this delicate valance!

DESIGNS BY ALIDA MACOR

Skill Level

Intermediate

Size

Seven-Panel Valance: 32 inches W x 11 inches H, including brass rings

Tie back: 23½ inches W x 1⅝ inches H, including plastic rings

Materials

- 4 sheets regular 7-count plastic canvas
- ⅓ vertical length artist-size sheet soft 7-count plastic canvas
- Uniek Needloft plastic canvas yarn as listed in color key
- Uniek Needloft metallic craft cord as listed in color key
- DMC #3 pearl cotton as listed in color key
- #16 tapestry needle
- 8 brass clip-on café rings
- 2 (1-inch) white plastic rings

Project Notes

With the exception of color keys, instructions and amounts given are for seven panels and two tiebacks. Plastic canvas and accessories will need to be adjusted for additional panels and tiebacks. Yardage given in each of the panel color keys is for one panel; yardage in tiebacks color key is for two tiebacks; a generous amount for Overcasting and Whipstitching is included in all keys.

For three panels, multiply yardage by

three; for two panels, multiply yardage by two, etc., keeping in mind the yardage given includes what it would take to Overcast one individual panel. To Overcast long edges with a single length of yarn, begin in the middle and work half the yarn in one direction. Turn project over and work remaining half of yarn in opposite direction.

Instructions

1. Following graphs throughout, cut seven valance panels from regular plastic canvas. Cut two 146-hole x 10-hole tiebacks from soft plastic canvas according to graphs (page 119), joining left and right halves before cutting. Do not repeat middle bar.

2. Stitch pieces following graphs and project note, being careful to begin and end stitching so tails will not be seen behind unstitched areas of canvas.

3. Stitch borders on all panels following panel graph given. Stitch three center motifs for panel A as shown on panel graph. Stitch two center motifs each for panels B and C (page 118) in shaded blue area.

4. Using white throughout, Whipstitch panels together in order shown in photo. Overcast side and top edges. **Note:** If following instructions in project note, use about a 3½-yard length white yarn for Overcasting.

5. Place a brass clip-on ring along top edge where each panel is joined together and at each end of assembled valance.

6. Using white, Overcast tiebacks in every other hole, catching a plastic ring at each

end. **Note:** If following instructions in project note, use about a 2½-yard length white yarn for Overcasting tieback.

7. Wrap tiebacks around curtains, then use white yarn to tie rings together. ●

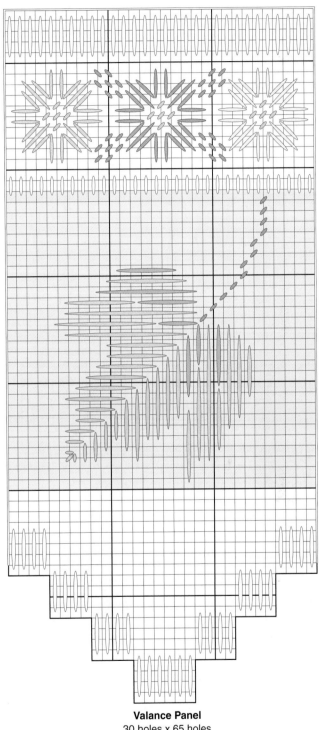

Valance Panel
30 holes x 65 holes
Cut 7 from regular
Stitch 3 as graphed for panel A
Stitch 2 each replacing center motif
with motifs for panels B and C

COLOR KEY	
PANEL A	
Plastic Canvas Yarn	**Yards**
☐ Tangerine #11	3
◪ Pumpkin #12	1
☐ Lemon #20	1
◪ Fern #23	1
☐ White #41	6
▨ Watermelon #55	1
☐ Yellow #57	1
Metallic Craft Cord	
☐ White/gold #55007	1
#3 Pearl Cotton	
▦ Ultra very dark topaz	1
Color numbers given are for Uniek Needloft plastic canvas yarn and metallic craft cord and DMC #3 pearl cotton.	

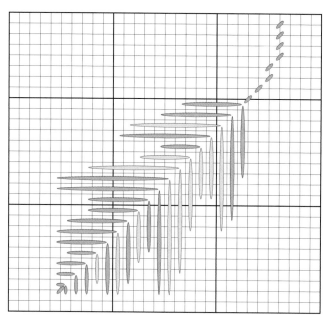

COLOR KEY
PANEL B

Plastic Canvas Yarn	Yards
☐ Tangerine #11	2
■ Pumpkin #12	2
☐ Lemon #20	1
■ Fern #23	1
☐ White #41	6

Metallic Craft Cord

☐ White/gold #55007	1

#3 Pearl Cotton

■ Ultra very dark topaz	1

Color numbers given are for Uniek
Needloft plastic canvas yarn and
metallic craft cord and DMC #3
pearl cotton.

Panel B Motif
Stitch 2

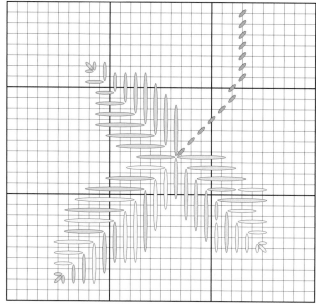

COLOR KEY
PANEL C

Plastic Canvas Yarn	Yards
☐ Tangerine #11	2
■ Pumpkin #12	2
☐ Lemon #20	3
■ Fern #23	1
☐ Moss #25	1
☐ White #41	6
☐ Yellow #57	2

Metallic Craft Cord

☐ White/gold #55007	1

#3 Pearl Cotton

■ Ultra very dark topaz	1

Color numbers given are for Uniek
Needloft plastic canvas yarn and
metallic craft cord and DMC #3
pearl cotton.

Panel C Motif
Stitch 2

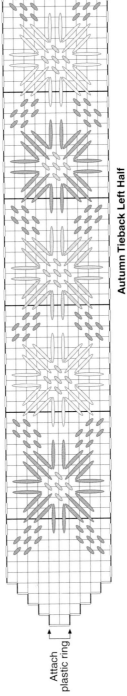

Middle Bar →

Attach plastic ring

Autumn Tieback Left Half
146 holes x 10 holes
Cut 2 from soft
Join with right half before cutting
Do not repeat middle bar

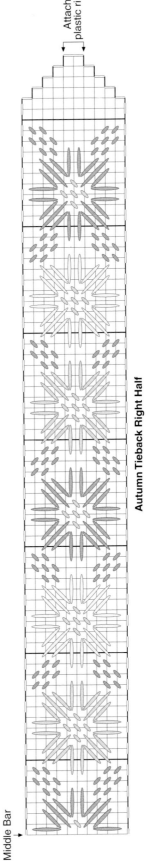

Attach plastic ring

Middle Bar →

Autumn Tieback Right Half
146 holes x 10 holes
Cut 2 from soft
Join with left half before cutting
Do not repeat middle bar

COLOR KEY
TIEBACKS

Plastic Canvas Yarn	Yards
☐ Tangerine #11	6
■ Pumpkin #12	8
☐ Lemon #20	6
■ Fern #23	11
✎ White #41 Overcasting	5
Metallic Craft Cord	
☐ White/gold #55007	7

Color numbers given are for Uniek
Needloft plastic canvas yarn and
metallic craft cord.

Country Crow

Fancy and festive, this cute little crow helps your autumn decor take wing!

DESIGN BY SUSAN LEINBERGER

Cutting & Stitching

1. Cut five body pieces and two wings from black plastic canvas, six legs pieces and three leg platform pieces from yellow plastic canvas and three beak pieces from clear plastic canvas according to graphs (page 122).

2. Stitch body and wing pieces with black following graphs, working eyes on one body piece only, completing the pattern stitch on remaining four pieces. When background stitching is completed, work black pearl cotton Backstitches on eyes.

3. Whipstitch body pieces together along side edges from dot to dot, easing as necessary to fit along angled edges. Do not Overcast wings and bottom edges of body.

4. For each leg, place three pieces together and stitch as one following graph. Place three leg platform pieces together and stitch as one, using three pattern stitches indicated on each side of platform to attach top edge of legs to platform while stitching. Do not Overcast edges.

5. Stitch beak pieces, working black stitches on beak top only; stitch bottom and back entirely with yellow.

6. Using yellow, Overcast front edges of top and bottom pieces. With wrong sides together, Whipstitch remaining two edges of beak top to two edges of beak back, then Whipstitch remaining two edges of beak bottom to remaining two edges of beak back.

Final Assembly

1. Using photo as a guide throughout final assembly, glue beak, wings, two sunflowers and two leaves to assembled body.

2. Cut an 18-inch x 1-inch length from red gingham fabric and fray edges slightly. Tie in a bow; trim and notch ends. Glue bow to crow below beak.

3. Cut a length of fabric to fit around straw hat for hat band; glue in place. Glue remaining sunflower and leaf to hat where ends of hat band meet.

4. Thread a 1-yard length of yellow yarn from bottom to top through center hole of leg platform, securing end with a knot.

5. Thread other end of yellow yarn through top of assembled crow and up through top of hat. Make a hanging loop and knot tightly at top of hat, then bring excess yarn back down through hat. Glue hat to top of crow.

6. Thread one length chenille stem through each hole at bottom of legs, bend in half and twist together for toes. ●

Skill Level

Intermediate

Size

10½ inches W x 17½ inches H, excluding hanger

Materials

- 1½ sheets black 7-count plastic canvas
- ½ sheet yellow 7-count plastic canvas
- ¼ sheet clear 7-count plastic canvas
- Uniek Needloft plastic canvas yarn as listed in color key
- #3 pearl cotton as listed in color key
- #16 tapestry needle
- Scraps red gingham fabric
- 6-inch straw doll hat
- 3 miniature silk sunflowers and leaves
- 6 (3-inch) lengths yellow chenille stem
- Hot-glue gun

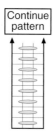

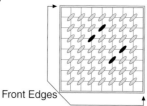

Continue pattern

Crow Leg
3 holes x 48 holes
Cut 6 from yellow

Attach to leg   Attach to leg

Crow Leg Platform
19 holes x 3 holes
Cut 3 from yellow

Front Edges

Crow Beak Top, Bottom & Back
8 holes x 8 holes
Cut 3 from clear
Stitch top as graphed
Stitch bottom and back
entirely with yellow

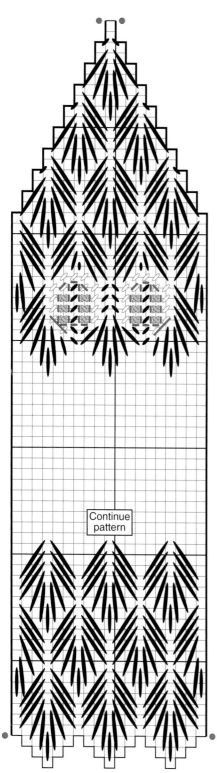

Continue pattern

Continue pattern

Crow Body
19 holes x 70 holes
Cut 5 from black
Stitch 1 as graphed
Stitch 4 entirely in pattern stitch

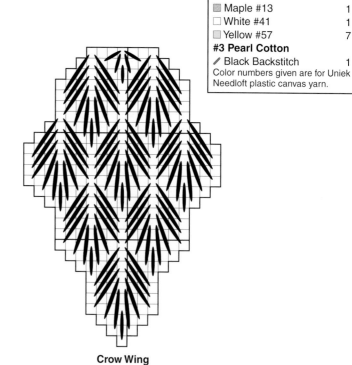

Crow Wing
19 holes x 28 holes
Cut 2 from black

COLOR KEY

Plastic Canvas Yarn	Yards
■ Black #00	80
▨ Maple #13	1
□ White #41	1
▨ Yellow #57	7
#3 Pearl Cotton	
╱ Black Backstitch	1

Color numbers given are for Uniek
Needloft plastic canvas yarn.

Dragonfly Pin

Dress up your autumn wardrobe with a dash of dragonfly dazzle!

DESIGN BY ROBIN PETRINA

Skill Level
Beginner

Size
1 ½ inches W x 1 ½ inches H

Materials
- Small amount 7-count plastic canvas
- Darice metallic cord as listed in color key
- #16 tapestry needle
- ¾-inch pin back
- Hot-glue gun

Instructions

1. Cut plastic canvas according to graph, carefully cutting apart wings along green lines and making sure to keep intact at red circles.

2. Overcast body with multi black and wings with multi white.

3. Glue pin back to body at wings. ●

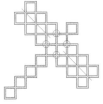

Pin Dragonfly
9 holes x 9 holes
Cut 1

COLOR KEY	
Metallic Cord	**Yards**
✎ Multi white #34021-108 Overcasting	1
✎ Multi black #34021-109 Overcasting	1
Color numbers given are for Darice metallic cord.	

Autumn Bug Welcome

This cheerful critter smiles through chubby cheeks as he offers your guests a share of this "fruitful" harvest!

DESIGN BY JANELLE GIESE

Project Notes

The triangle, heart, star, square, inverted triangle and diamond shapes designate Continental Stitches.

The sign graph is shared with the other bug welcome designs in other chapters of this book. Colors used for each season are given with the graphs and/or the instructions for that season.

Instructions

1. Cut bug (page 126) and sign (page 34) from plastic canvas according to graphs.

2. Stitch and Overcast welcome sign following graph, working uncoded background with eggshell Continental Stitches; replace lavender yarn with rust yarn.

3. When background stitching on sign is completed, work orange heavy braid Straight Stitches over rust yarn Continental Stitches. Using black #3 pearl cotton, embroider remaining portions of lettering.

4. Stitch and Overcast bug, working uncoded areas on face and body with baby yellow Continental Stitches and uncoded areas on tree bark with cinnamon Continental Stitches.

5. When background stitching is completed, embroider orange braid accents on wings; work both #3 and #5 black pearl cotton embroidery, leaving apple stem unworked at this time.

6. Use a full strand white yarn to Straight Stitch eye and antennae highlights; use full strand cinnamon to Straight Stitch apple stem, then work #3 pearl cotton Straight Stitch to the right of cinnamon stem.

7. Sew sawtooth hanger to top center back of bug's head with #5 pearl cotton. Using needle-nose pliers, join bug to sign by forming two chains of three jump rings each, attaching top and bottom jump rings through holes indicated with blue dots. ●

Skill Level

Advanced

Size

8 inches W x 13¼ inches H

Materials

- 1 sheet stiff 7-count plastic canvas
- Uniek Needloft plastic canvas yarn as listed in color key
- Kreinik Heavy (#32) Braid as listed in color key
- #5 pearl cotton as listed in color key
- #3 pearl cotton as listed in color key
- #16 tapestry needle
- Sawtooth hanger
- 6 (7mm) nickel jump rings
- Needle-nose pliers

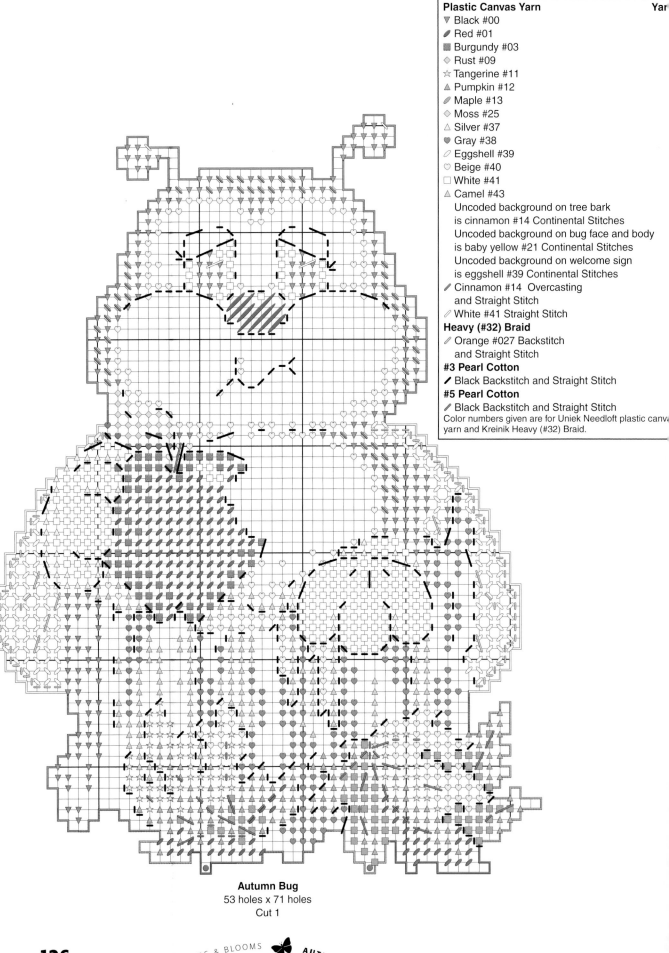

COLOR KEY

Plastic Canvas Yarn

▽	Black #00
▰	Red #01
▣	Burgundy #03
◇	Rust #09
☆	Tangerine #11
△	Pumpkin #12
▱	Maple #13
◇	Moss #25
△	Silver #37
♥	Gray #38
◖	Eggshell #39
♡	Beige #40
□	White #41
△	Camel #43

Uncoded background on tree bark
is cinnamon #14 Continental Stitches
Uncoded background on bug face and body
is baby yellow #21 Continental Stitches
Uncoded background on welcome sign
is eggshell #39 Continental Stitches

▱ Cinnamon #14 Overcasting
and Straight Stitch
▱ White #41 Straight Stitch

Heavy (#32) Braid
▱ Orange #027 Backstitch
and Straight Stitch

#3 Pearl Cotton
▱ Black Backstitch and Straight Stitch

#5 Pearl Cotton
▱ Black Backstitch and Straight Stitch

Color numbers given are for Uniek Needloft plastic canva
yarn and Kreinik Heavy (#32) Braid.

Autumn Bug
53 holes x 71 holes
Cut 1

Mystic Butterfly Candle Platform

Majestic and marvelous, this elegant accent twinkles with the spirit of starry fall evenings!

DESIGN BY JANELLE GIESE

Skill Level
Advanced

Size
4 inches H x 5 1/2 inches in diameter

Materials
- 1 sheet black 7-count plastic canvas
- 2 (4-inch) Uniek QuickShape plastic canvas radial circles
- Coats & Clark Red Heart Classic worsted weight yarn Art. E267 as listed in color key
- Kreinik Heavy (#32) Braid as listed in color key
- #3 pearl cotton as listed in color key
- #16 tapestry needle
- 1 1/2 cups aquarium gravel
- 5-inch square black felt
- Thick white glue

Project Notes
Please use caution. Plastic canvas and yarn will melt and burn if it gets too hot or comes in contact with a flame. Never leave a lit candle unattended. Recommended for decorative purposes only.

Use 2 strands gold braid when working Continental Stitches; use 1 strand for all other gold braid stitching.

Cutting & Stitching
1. Cut one side and three single butterflies from plastic canvas according to graphs (page 128). Cut outermost row of holes from each plastic canvas radial circle (not graphed) for platform top and base. Base will remain unstitched.

2. Cut felt slightly smaller all around than base.

3. Continental Stitch top with black; work a Cross Stitch in center.

4. Stitch single butterflies following graph, working uncoded background with black Continental Stitches. Overcast wings. Do not Overcast body edges.

5. Using a full strand yarn, work white and copper Straight Stitches on upper wings and country blue French Knots on lower wings, wrapping needle one time.

6. Work black pearl cotton embroidery shown on single butterfly graph, wrapping pearl cotton around country blue French Knots, coming up and going down at the same point (not graphed).

7. Stitch side following graph, overlapping six holes before stitching and working uncoded background with black Continental Stitches. Do not stitch red and blue highlighted lines and shaded yellow areas.

8. Work gold braid embroidery on side,

wrapping needle one time for French Knots.

Assembly

1. To Whipstitch platform top to side, use Continental Stitches and Cross Stitches in colors indicated on red lines and black along top edges of side. Top will seem slightly large. Ease to fit by Whipstitching an extra hole on top to side at spaces between butterflies. Overcast edge of top only behind bodies of butterflies.

CONTINUED ON PAGE 135

Body Embroidery Diagram

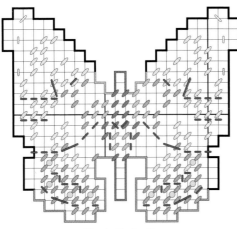

Single Butterfly
23 holes x 20 holes
Cut 3

COLOR KEY
Worsted Weight Yarn	Yards
▨ Bronze #286	5
☐ Copper #289	4
▨ Mid brown #339	2
■ Coffee #365	2
☐ Nickel #401	1
▨ Claret #762	9
■ Windsor blue #808	4
Uncoded areas on white backgrounds are black #12 Continental Stitches	
Black #12 Overcasting and Whipstitching	
╱ Off white #3 Straight Stitch	1
╱ Copper #289 Straight Stitch	
╱ Mid brown #339 Straight Stitch	
○ Country blue #882 French Knot	
Heavy (#32) Braid	
☐ Gold #002	10
╱ Gold #002 Backstitch and Straight Stitch	
○ Gold #002 French Knot	
#3 Pearl Cotton	
╱ Black Backstitch and Straight Stitch	5

Color numbers given are for Coats & Clark Red Heart Classic worsted weight yarn Art. E267 and Kreinik Heavy (#32) Braid.

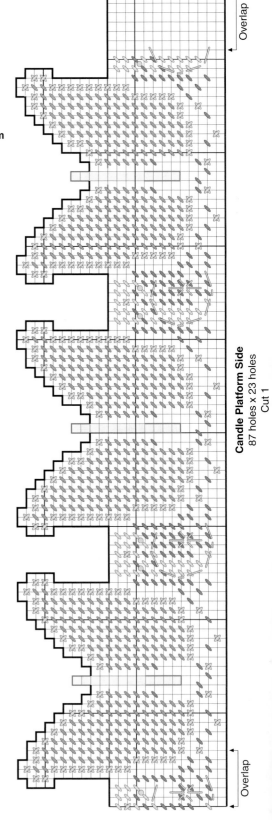

Candle Platform Side
87 holes x 23 holes
Cut 1

Overlap

Overlap

Dragonfly Box

With a hint of mystery and an aura of elegance, this dragonfly keepsake has a captivating charm!

DESIGN BY ROBIN PETRINA

Instructions

1. Cut plastic canvas according to graphs (page 130), carefully cutting apart wings along red lines. Cut one 32-hole x 32-hole piece for box bottom. Box bottom will remain unstitched.

2. Following graphs throughout, stitch and Overcast dragonfly. Stitch box and lid pieces.

3. Using dark plum throughout, Overcast top edges of box sides and bottom edges of lid sides from yellow dot to yellow dot. Whipstitch box sides together, then Whipstitch box sides to unstitched box bottom. Whipstitch lid sides together, then Whipstitch lid sides to lid top.

4. Glue dragonfly to lid top (see photo). ●

Skill Level

Beginner

Size

5¼ inches square x 2⅞ inches H

Materials

- 1 sheet 7-count plastic canvas
- Coats & Clark Red Heart Super Saver worsted weight yarn Art. E300 as listed in color key
- #16 tapestry needle
- Hot-glue gun

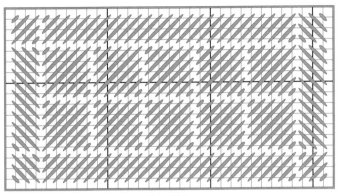

Box Side
32 holes x 17 holes
Cut 4

COLOR KEY

Worsted Weight Yarn		Yards
☐ Soft white #316		2
■ Dark plum #533		45
☐ Light sage #631		1
⁄ Light sage #631 Backstitch		

Color numbers given are for Coats & Clark Red Heart Super Saver worsted weight yarn Art. E300.

Box Dragonfly
24 holes x 24 holes
Cut 1

Lid Side
34 holes x 4 holes
Cut 4

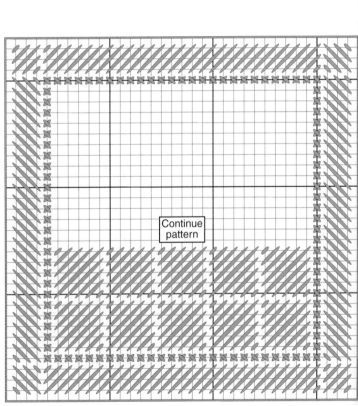

Continue pattern

Lid Top
34 holes x 34 holes
Cut 1

Ladybug Photo Album

It's easy to "spot" your favorite photos
with this lovely ladybug album!

DESIGN BY SUE PENROD

Album Cover

1. Cut front and back from plastic canvas
according to graph (page 132).
2. Stitch and Overcast front following
graph, working uncoded areas with black
Continental Stitches. Stitch entire back
with black Continental Stitches; Overcast
with black.
3. When background stitching and
Overcasting are completed, embroider
front using 3-ply floss to work black and
white Backstitches and French Knots. Use
6-ply floss to work red French Knot.

Album Pages

1. Fold 9-inch square black construction
paper in quarters (photo 1).
2. Keeping paper folded, place point of
ladybug back on folded corner of paper;
trace heart shape.
3. Keeping paper folded, cut out shape,
making rounded edges slightly smaller
(photo 2).

4. Fold paper in half widthwise (photo 3)
so that two opposite hearts are folded in
half. Fold these hearts to inside (photo 4).
Do not fold remaining hearts.
5. Trace around folded heart two times
on 6½-inch x 3½-inch piece of construction paper; cut out slightly smaller all
around, then cut one heart shape in half.
These patterns will be used to cut photo-
graph shapes.

Assembly

1. With wrong sides up, lay album cover
pieces point to point, then glue ribbon
over middle of each piece, making ends
even. Allow to dry.
2. One at a time, glue unfolded heart
shapes over ribbon to wrong sides of
front and back; allow to dry.
3. Using pattern pieces, cut photos and
attach with double-sided tape. ●

Skill Level

Beginner

Size

3 inches W x 3 inches H

Materials

- ¼ sheet 7-count plastic canvas
- Worsted weight yarn as listed in color key
- 6-strand embroidery floss as listed in
  color key
- #16 tapestry needle
- Black construction paper:
  9-inch square
  6½-inch x 3½-inch piece
- 14 inches ¼-inch-wide black satin ribbon
- Double-sided adhesive tape
- Tacky craft glue

1

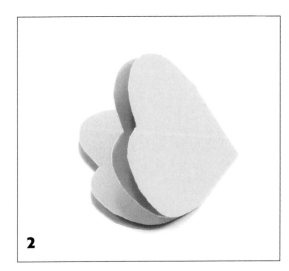

2

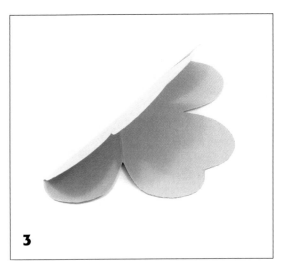

3

4

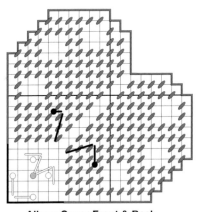

Album Cover Front & Back
18 holes x 18 holes
Cut 2
Stitch front as graphed
Stitch back entirely with
black Continental Stitches

Mallard Frame

Display your autumn photos in this masculine-looking frame.

DESIGN BY MARY T. COSGROVE

Instructions

1. Cut frame front and back from plastic canvas according to graphs (pages 134 and 135), cutting out opening for photo insertion on frame back. Frame back will remain unstitched.

2. Stitch frame front following graph, working uncoded areas with rust Continental Stitches; Overcast inside edges with brown.

3. When background stitching is completed, work brown Backstitches and chartreuse and turquoise French Knots.

4. Whipstitch frame front and back together with brown.

5. Select two groups of leaf foliage from pressed flowers. Apply decoupage medium to both sides of leaves. Place one group on lower left corner of frame front and one above mallard on the right. ●

Skill Level

Beginner

Size

6⅛ inches W x 6⅛ inches H; opening approximately 3¾ inches W x 3¾ inches H

Materials

- 1 sheet 7-count plastic canvas
- Uniek Needloft plastic canvas as listed in color key
- Kreinik ⅛-Inch Ribbon as listed in color key
- #16 tapestry needle
- 8 (6-inch) lengths lilac craft wire
- Glossy decoupage medium
- All Night Media Embellishments Blue/Purple Mix #77BLU pressed flowers by Plaid

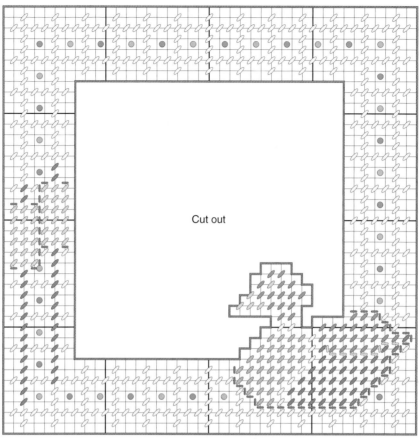

Mallard Frame Front
40 holes x 40 holes
Cut 1

COLOR KEY

Plastic Canvas Yarn	Yards
■ Brown #15	6
☐ Flesh tone #56	8
Uncoded areas are rust #09 Continental Stitches	6
╱ Brown #15 Backstitch	
¹/₈-Inch Ribbon	
☐ Vintage gold #002V	2
▨ Chartreuse #015	2
■ Turquiose #029	3
● Chartreuse #015 French Knot	
● Turquiose #029 French Knot	

Color numbers given are for Uniek Needloft plastic canvas yarn and Kreinik ¹/₈-Inch Ribbon.

Top Edge

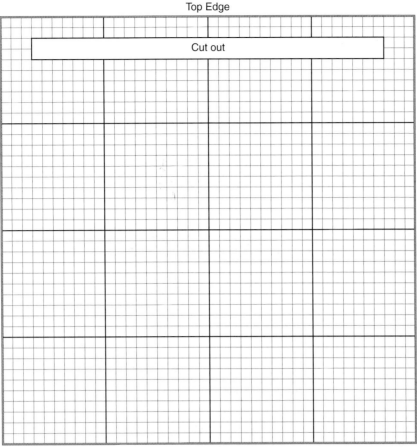

Mallard Frame Back
40 holes x 40 holes
Cut 1
Do not stitch

MYSTIC BUTTERFLY CANDLE PLATFORM CONTINUED FROM PAGE 128

2. Overcast top portion of wings. Do not Overcast head portion of body.

3. Place single butterflies over butterflies on side, matching body edges of single butterflies with blue lines on side. Whipstitch head and tail portions together with coffee.

4. Following body embroidery diagram, work two vertical mid brown Straight Stitches first, then work gold braid vertical and diagonal Straight Stitches. Work pearl cotton horizontal Straight Stitches last.

5. Using black, Whipstitch base to bottom edge of side, filling with aquarium gravel before closing.

6. For antennae, thread black pearl cotton into top of each butterfly at one side of head, leaving a ¾-inch tail. Make a small stitch at back of stitching to anchor, then bring pearl cotton out on other side at top of head, again leaving a ¾-inch tail. Stiffen antennae with glue between fingers; allow to dry.

7. Glue felt to base; allow to dry. ●

Winter

Snowfalls and sledding, parties and presents—these are the joyous delights of winter! Our warm-hearted array of cold-weather projects gives you plenty of reasons to welcome the season!

Partridge in a Pear Tree Wreath

Be a "true love" to your guests on every day of the Christmas season with this fruit-filled partridge wreath!

DESIGN BY KATHLEEN HURLEY

Instructions

1. Cut plastic canvas according to graphs (this page and pages 138 and 139).

2. Stitch and Overcast pieces following graphs, working uncoded areas with Continental Stitches as follows: white background with cinnamon, blue background with flesh tone and yellow background with yellow.

3. Using photo as a guide through step 4, thread ends of metallic cord through back of stitching on each end of banner until banner hangs in center about 3¼ inches from wreath. Knot ends and trim. Tack or glue center of cord to wreath front.

4. Tack or glue partridges and pears to wreath. ●

Skill Level

Beginner

Size

Right-Facing Partridge: 6⅞ inches W x 9½ inches H

Left-Facing Partridge: 7⅞ inches W x 8¼ inches H

Welcome Banner: 8⅞ inches W x 5⅜ inches H, excluding hanger

Double Pears: 4½ inches W x 5½ inches H

Single Pear: 3¾ inches W x 3⅞ inches H

Materials

- 2 sheets 7-count plastic canvas
- Uniek Needloft plastic canvas yarn as listed in color key
- #16 tapestry needle
- 16-inch straw wreath
- 18 inches red metallic cord
- Hot-glue gun (optional)

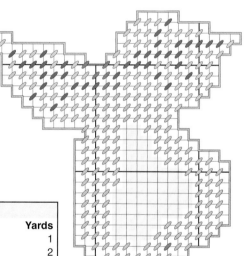

Wreath Single Pear
24 holes x 25 holes
Cut 2

COLOR KEY	
Plastic Canvas Yarn	**Yards**
■ Black #00	1
▨ Red #01	2
▨ Burgundy #03	1
☐ Pink #07	2
☐ Tangerine #11	30
☐ Fern #23	26
■ Holly #27	13
☐ Gray #38	6
☐ White #41	13
☐ Camel #43	13
Uncoded areas with white background are cinnamon #14 Continental Stitches	8
Uncoded areas with blue background are flesh tone #56 Continental Stitches	2
Uncoded areas with yellow background are yellow #57 Continental Stitches	15
╱ Cinnamon #14 Overcasting	
Color numbers given are for Uniek Needloft plastic canvas yarn.	

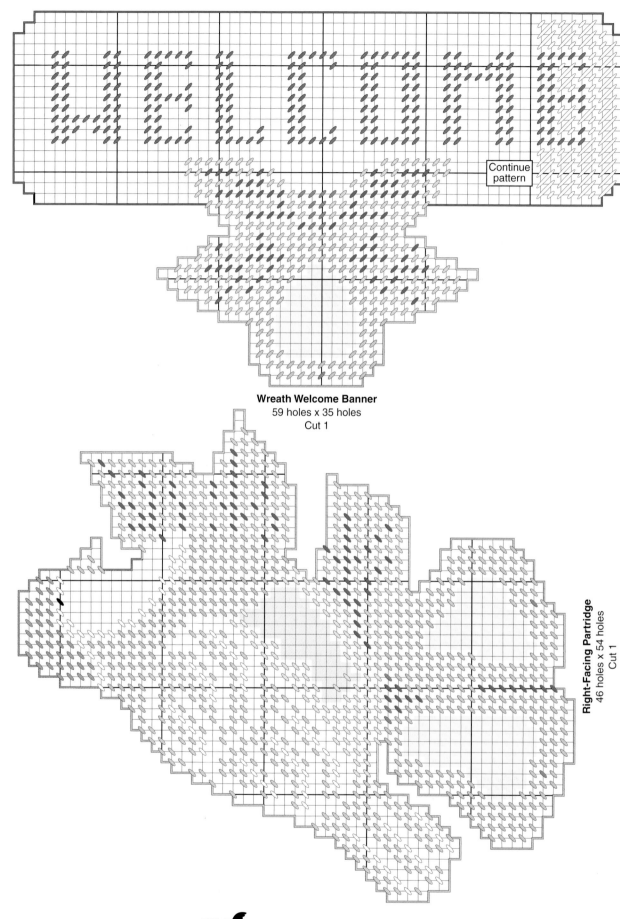

Wreath Welcome Banner
59 holes x 35 holes
Cut 1

Right-Facing Partridge
46 holes x 54 holes
Cut 1

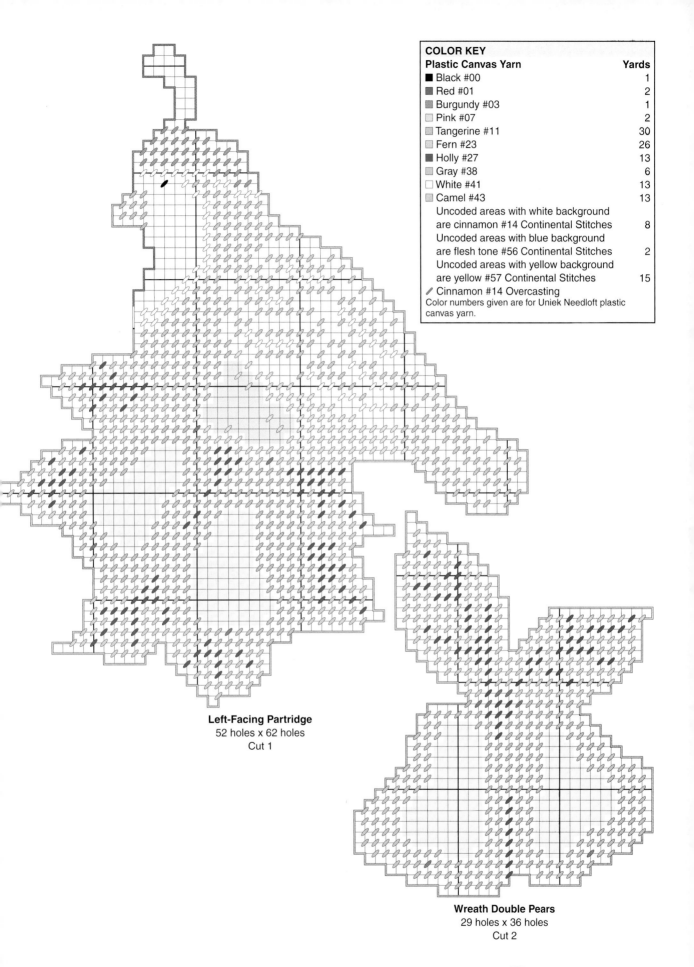

COLOR KEY

Plastic Canvas Yarn	Yards
■ Black #00	1
■ Red #01	2
■ Burgundy #03	1
□ Pink #07	2
□ Tangerine #11	30
□ Fern #23	26
■ Holly #27	13
■ Gray #38	6
□ White #41	13
□ Camel #43	13
Uncoded areas with white background are cinnamon #14 Continental Stitches	8
Uncoded areas with blue background are flesh tone #56 Continental Stitches	2
Uncoded areas with yellow background are yellow #57 Continental Stitches	15
∕ Cinnamon #14 Overcasting	

Color numbers given are for Uniek Needloft plastic canvas yarn.

Left-Facing Partridge
52 holes x 62 holes
Cut 1

Wreath Double Pears
29 holes x 36 holes
Cut 2

Winter Dragonfly

Sparkling with the delicate beauty of a snowflake, this delightful dragonfly is sure to please!

DESIGN BY PAM BULL

Skill Level
Beginner

Size
5½ inches W x 3³⁄₈ inches H, excluding raffia bow

Materials
- ¼ sheet 10-count plastic canvas
- DMC 6-strand embroidery floss as listed in color key
- #18 tapestry needle
- 2 (7mm) movable eyes
- 1-yard-long strands raffia
- 6-inches ivory twisted paper ribbon
- 5 (1-inch) snowflake shapes as desired (see project note)
- Hot-glue gun

Project Note
Snowflake punch was used in sample to make snowflakes with two different shades of blue paper.

Instructions
1. Cut plastic canvas according to graphs.
2. Stitch and Overcast pieces following graphs, working medium blue violet "spots" on wings following Fig. 1.
3. When background stitching is completed, work black Backstitches with 3-ply black.

4. Using photo as a guide through step 7, untwist paper ribbon, gather in center to form a bow and tie with ecru floss.
5. Glue body to center of wings, then glue assembled dragonfly at an angle over center of paper ribbon bow.
6. Glue snowflake shapes to wings. Glue eyes to top of head.
7. Tie several strands raffia in a 4³⁄₄-inch-wide bow, leaving long tails. Glue twisted paper to tails approximately 2½ inches from bow. Trim raffia tails as desired. ●

Winter Dragonfly Body
7 holes x 33 holes
Cut 1

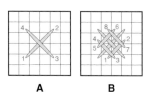

A   B

Fig. 1
Work large Cross Stitch in graph A,
coming up at 1, down at 2,
up at 3, down at 4
Continue stitching following graph B,
coming up at 1, down at 2, etc.

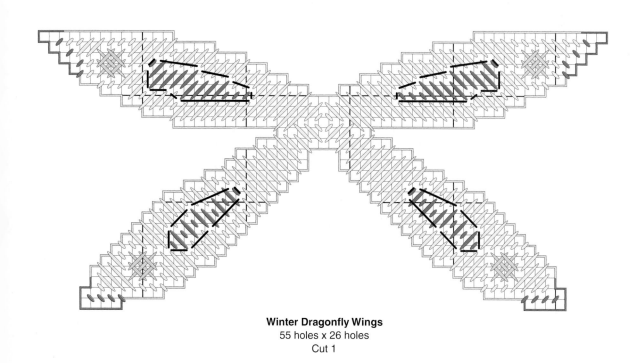

Winter Dragonfly Wings
55 holes x 26 holes
Cut 1

Poinsettia Tissue Topper

Brilliant berries and pine green leaves adorn the snowy sides of this gorgeous topper!

DESIGN BY JOYCE MESSENGER

Skill Level

Intermediate

Size

Fits boutique-style tissue topper

Materials

- 2½ sheets 7-count plastic canvas
- Worsted weight yarn as listed in color key
- #16 tapestry needle
- 10 (7mm) dark yellow transparent beads
- Yellow #5 pearl cotton to match beads

Instructions

1. Cut plastic canvas according to graphs.

2. Stitch topper pieces following graphs, working forest green leaves with Continental Stitches, Reverse Continental Stitches and Slanted Gobelin Stitches first, then filling in with rows of white Slanted Gobelin Stitches.

3. When background stitching is completed, work forest green Backstitches and Straight Stitches, then add red French Knots.

4. Stitch and Overcast poinsettia petals following graphs.

5. For each poinsettia, put two corresponding petal pieces together so petals of top layer are between petals of bottom layer; tack together in center with red yarn.

6. Using yellow pearl cotton, attach four beads to center of large poinsettia and three beads to center of each small poinsettia.

7. Using photo as a guide and red yarn, tack assembled poinsettias to one side, placing large poinsettia at bottom right.

8. Using white, Whipstitch sides together, then Whipstitch sides to top. Overcast inside edges of top and bottom edges of sides with forest green. ●

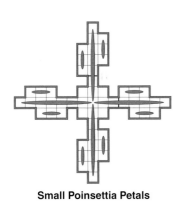

Small Poinsettia Petals
15 holes x 15 holes
Cut 4

Large Poinsettia Petals
19 holes x 19 holes
Cut 2

COLOR KEY

Worsted Weight Yarn	Yards
☐ White	62
■ Forest green	29
■ Red	18
╱ Forest green Backstitch and Straight Stitch	
● Red French Knot	

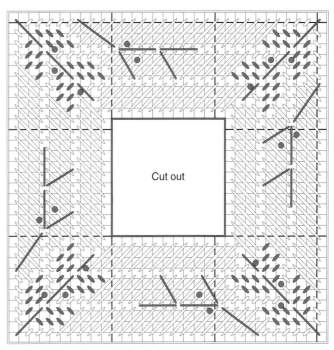

Poinsettia Topper Top
31 holes x 31 holes
Cut 1

Cut out

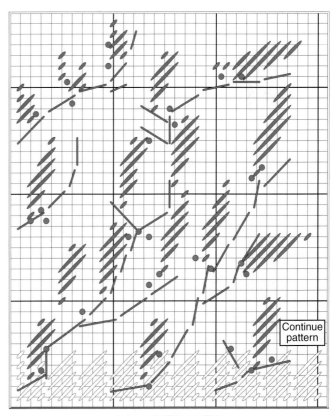

Continue pattern

Poinsettia Topper Side
31 holes x 37 holes
Cut 4

Cardinal

Perched on a pine bough and plumped for the winter, this brilliant bird brings colorful cheer!

DESIGN BY TERRY RICIOLI

Skill Level
Beginner

Size
6¹⁄₈ inches W x 7³⁄₈ inches H

Materials
- 1 sheet 7-count plastic canvas
- Uniek Needloft plastic canvas yarn as listed in color key
- #16 tapestry needle
- 6mm black cabochon
- Hot-glue gun

Instructions

1. Cut plastic canvas according to graphs.

2. Stitch and Overcast pieces following graphs, working uncoded background on front with baby blue Continental Stitches and leaving center area of plaque back unworked as shown.

3. When background stitching is completed, work black Straight Stitches for birds feet and forest Straight Stitches for pine needles.

4. Glue cabochon to head for eye where indicated on graph. Center and glue front over unstitched area on back.

5. Hang as desired. ●

COLOR KEY	
Plastic Canvas Yarn	**Yard**
■ Black #00	
■ Red #01	
☐ Christmas red #02	
■ Burgundy #03	
▨ Pumpkin #12	
■ Brown #15	
☐ Sandstone #16	
Uncoded background on front is baby blue #36 Continental Stiches	
⁄ Baby blue #36 Overcasting	
✁ Black #00 Straight Stitch	
✁ Forest #29 Straight Stitch	
● Attach black cabochon	
Color numbers given are for Uniek Needloft plastic canvas yarn.	

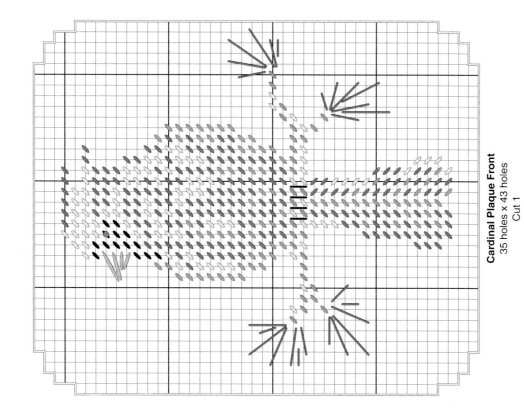

Cardinal Plaque Front
35 holes x 43 holes
Cut 1

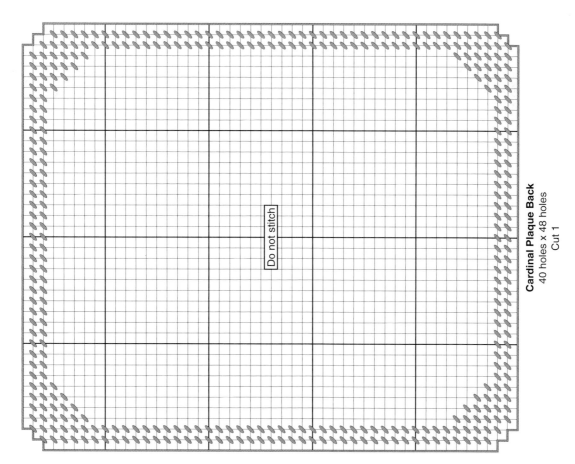

Do not stitch

Cardinal Plaque Back
40 holes x 48 holes
Cut 1

Chickadee

This winged warbler will warm your heart throughout the winter months!

DESIGN BY TERRY RICIOLI

Skill Level

Beginner

Size

7³⁄₈ inches W x 6¹⁄₈ inches H

Materials

- 1 sheet 7-count plastic canvas
- Uniek Needloft plastic canvas yarn as listed in color key
- #16 tapestry needle
- 6mm black cabochon
- Hot-glue gun

Instructions

1. Cut plastic canvas according to graphs.

2. Stitch and Overcast pieces following graphs, leaving center area of plaque back unworked as shown.

3. Glue cabochon to head for eye where indicated on graph. Center and glue front over unstitched area on back.

4. Hang as desired. ●

COLOR KEY	
Plastic Canvas Yarn	**Yards**
■ Black #00	1
▨ Brown #15	20
☐ Sandstone #16	4
☐ Baby blue #36	20
▨ Gray #38	3
☐ White #41	1
● Attach black cabochon	
Color numbers given are for Uniek Needloft plastic canvas yarn.	

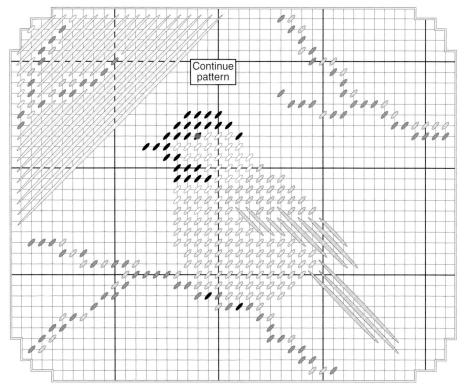

Chickadee Plaque Front
43 holes x 35 holes
Cut 1

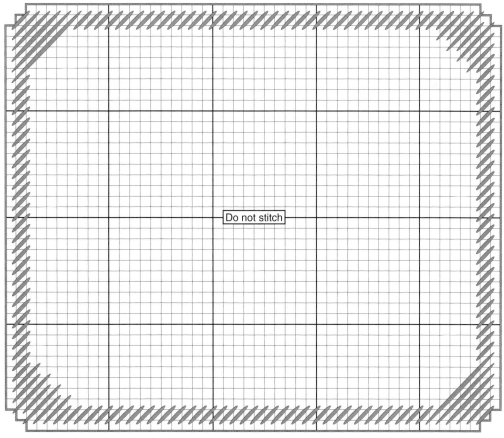

Chickadee Plaque Back
48 holes x 40 holes
Cut 1

Winter Floral Match Box

Dainty and demure, this tapestry box is right at home by the fireplace!

DESIGN BY JANELLE GIESE

Skill Level
Advanced

Size
2³/₈ inches W x 12 inches H x
2³/₈ inches D

Materials
- 1¼ sheet stiff 7-count plastic canvas
- Coats & Clark Red Heart Classic worsted weight yarn Art. E267 as listed in color key
- Elmore-Pisgah Inc. Honeysuckle rayon chenille yarn as listed in color key
- Kreinik Medium (#16) Braid as listed in color key
- Kreinik Tapestry (#12) Braid as listed in color key
- #16 tapestry needle
- Box purchased fireplace matches

Project Notes

When stitching with chenille yarn, use double strands, placing strands together into needle. **Always** work in direction of nap. Yarn falls apart and knots if worked against nap. To find direction of nap, draw a strand between fingers near knuckles.

Cutting

1. Cut one box front, one lid front, three box side/back pieces and three lid side/back pieces from plastic canvas according to graphs (this page and page 150).

2. From plastic canvas, cut two 14-hole x 14-hole pieces for lid top and box base, four 12-hole x 1-hole pieces for lid rims and four 12-hole x 6-hole pieces for lid lips.

Fronts, Top & Base

1. Continental Stitch lid top and box base with baked apple.

2. Stitch lid front and box front following graphs, working uncoded background with tan Continental Stitches.

3. Overcast top edge of box front; center and Whipstitch bottom edge of lid front to one lid rim, using Continental Stitches as indicated.

4. Using full strand yarn, work claret Backstitches on berries and warm brown Backstitches at tip of branch on lid front. Use 1-ply country blue on flower petals; on leaves, use 2-ply yarn for tan and light sage Straight Stitches.

5. Backstitch features of flowers using tapestry braid and borders using medium braid.

Sides & Backs

1. Work baked apple Continental Stitches on box sides and back and on lid sides and back.

2. Prepare woodsy ombre yarn as follows: Pull strand from ball and make first cut at beginning of dark green shade. Strand should follow a pattern of dark green to light green to beige to dark red. Make second cut where end of dark red meets dark green. Strand will measure about 1¾ yards.

3. Cut 38 strands. Place strands together in sets of two, aligning color segments. For each pair of strands, fold in half with ends even, then cut at fold which will be about center of ivory.

4. Fill in rows of Slanted Gobelin Stitches using prepared strands of woodsy ombre. While stitching, keep corresponding lid and box pieces together to create a complete row of colors.

5. Begin at top left stripe of one lid piece. Draw green end of two strands into needle. In working with nap, ivory ends will be the tail and the first stitch. Complete first stripe on lid piece, then continue working stripe on corresponding box piece, continuing down left stripe to end of yarn.

6. The next length of yarn will be ivory in your needle with a dark red tail, making dark red the first stitch. Continue working till end of yarn. Ivory will meet ivory when beginning the next pair of strands.

7. Continue filling in stripes with this method, following arrows of working direction (down left stripe, up middle stripes of box and lid, down right stripes of lid and box side). Repeat with remaining lid and box pieces.

8. Overcast top edges of box pieces. Center and Whipstitch top edge of one lid rim to bottom edge of each remaining lid piece using matching colors of chenille yarn. For stripe areas, match yarn colors; 1 ply may be stitched twice through each hole.

Final Assembly

1. Using baked apple through step 3, Whipstitch box front and back to box sides, then Whipstitch front, back and sides to box base.

2. Making sure to match lid pieces to their corresponding box pieces, Whipstitch lid front and back to lid sides, Whipstitching over corners between lid rims. Whipstitch lid, front, back and sides to lid top.

3. Whipstitch 6-hole edges of lid lips together, forming a square, then Whipstitch lips to lid rims, catching stitch at each corner of rim while working around square. Overcast bottom edges of lid lips.

4. Cut box of matches to 8½ inches high, then insert box and matches into completed project. ●

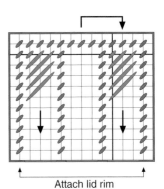

Attach lid rim

Lid Side/Back
14 holes x 12 holes
Cut 3
Stitch each with
corresponding box piece,
going down left row of lid then box,
up middle row of box then lid,
down right row of lid then box
Begin and end each yarn
length following instructions

COLOR KEY	
Rayon Chenille Yarn	**Yards**
■ Baked apple #24	80
■ Woodsy ombre #101	70
Worsted Weight Yarn	
□ White #1	2
□ Eggshell #111	3
▨ Cornmeal #220	1
▨ Tan #334	8
■ Warm brown #336	3
□ Silver #412	1
□ Light sage #631	3
■ Dark sage #633	1
Uncoded areas are tan #334 Continental Stitches	
⁄ Tan #334 (2-ply) Straight Stitch	
⁄ Warm brown #336 (4-ply) Backstitch	
⁄ Light sage #631 (2-ply) Straight Stitch	
⁄ Claret #762 (4-ply) Backstitch	1
⁄ Country blue #882 (1-ply) Straight Stitch	1
Medium (#16) Braid	
⁄ Antique gold #205C Backstitch	4
Tapestry (#12) Braid	
⁄ Antique gold #205C Backstitch and Straight Stitch	4
Color numbers given are for Elmore-Pisgah Honeysuckle rayon chenille yarn, Coats & Clark Red Heart Classic worsted weight yarn Art. E267 and Kreinik Medium (#16) and Tapestry (#12) braids.	

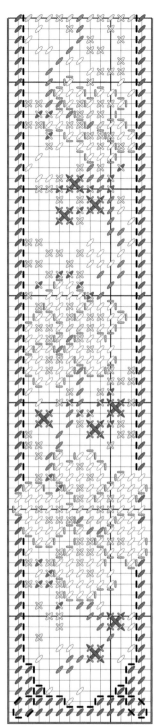

Box Front
14 holes x 66 holes
Cut 1

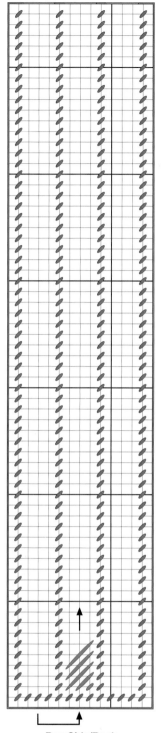

Box Side/Back
14 holes x 66 holes
Cut 3
Stitch each with
corresponding lid piece,
going down left row of lid then box,
up middle row of box then lid,
down right row of lid then box
Begin and end each yarn
length following instructions

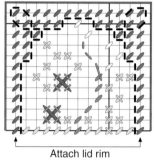

Attach lid rim

Lid Front
14 holes x 12 holes
Cut 1

COLOR KEY	
Rayon Chenille Yarn	**Yards**
■ Baked apple #24	80
■ Woodsy ombre #101	70
Worsted Weight Yarn	
☐ White #1	2
☐ Eggshell #111	3
☐ Cornmeal #220	1
☐ Tan #334	8
■ Warm brown #336	3
▨ Silver #412	1
☐ Light sage #631	3
■ Dark sage #633	1
Uncoded areas are tan #334 Continental Stitches	
╱ Tan #334 (2-ply) Straight Stitch	
╱ Warm brown #336 (4-ply) Backstitch	
╱ Light sage #631 (2-ply) Straight Stitch	
╱ Claret #762 (4-ply) Backstitch	1
╱ Country blue #882 (1-ply) Straight Stitch	1
Medium (#16) Braid	
╱ Antique gold #205C Backstitch	4
Tapestry (#12) Braid	
╱ Antique gold #205C Backstitch and Straight Stitch	4
Color numbers given are for Elmore-Pisgah Honeysuckle rayon chenille yarn, Coats & Clark Red Heart Classic worsted weight yarn Art. E267 and Kreinik Medium (#16) and Tapestry (#12) braids.	

Wineglass Rings

Garnish your glassware with these festive floral accents to "ring" in the New Year with style!

DESIGN BY SUE PENROD

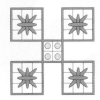

Skill Level

Beginner

Size

1¹⁄₈ inches W x 1¹⁄₈ inches H, excluding ring

Materials

- Small amount 10-count plastic canvas
- DMC 6-strand embroidery floss as listed in color key
- #18 tapestry needle
- 4 (1-inch) round stemware hoops/ear wires
- 4 (6mm) jump rings
- 8 (4mm) beads in colors as desired
- Needle-nose pliers

Flower Petals
8 holes x 8 holes
Cut 8
Stitch 1 with dark
seagreen as graphed
Stitch 1 each replacing dark
seagreen with peach,
bright red, light seagreen,
very dark mauve, mauve,
medium melon and
very dark melon

COLOR KEY	
6-Strand Embroidery Floss	**Yards**
Peach #353	1
Bright red #666	1
◼ Dark seagreen #958	1
Light seagreen #964	1
Very dark mauve #3685	1
Mauve #3687	1
Medium melon #3706	1
Very dark melon #3801	1
◯ Light tangerine #742	
(3-ply) French Knot	1
Color numbers given are for DMC 6-strand embroidery floss.	

Instructions

1. Cut two petal pieces for each flower set from plastic canvas according to graph for a total of eight pieces or four sets.
2. Stitch and Overcast pieces following graphs, working one each in medium melon, peach, very dark melon, bright red, mauve, very dark mauve, light seagreen and dark seagreen.
3. Using 3-ply light tangerine, work French Knots in center of medium melon, very dark melon, very dark mauve and dark seagreen petals.
4. Place petals together in sets as follows: medium melon and peach, very dark melon and bright red, very dark mauve and mauve, and light seagreen and dark seagreen.
5. Layer set pieces so that petals with French Knots are on top and petals are between petals of bottom layer. Carefully slip each petal on top layer between two petals on bottom layer until it locks in place. Now petals of top layer are bottom petals.
6. Using needle-nose pliers, for each flower, insert jump ring through hole on tip of one bottom petal; close jump ring.
7. Bend hook on stemware hoop slightly down then slip on one bead. Slip jump ring onto hoop, then slip on second bead.
8. Bend hook up, then hook to close. ●

Cardinal on a Stick

This fiery red flutterer brings mistletoe and merriment to all!

DESIGN BY KATHY WIRTH

Project Note

Use #16 tapestry needle with yarn and #24 tapestry needle with 6-strand embroidery floss.

Cutting & Stitching

1. Cut plastic canvas according to graphs (page 154).

2. Stitch leaves following graph. Stitch one cardinal as graphed; reverse remaining cardinal and stitch, working stitches in opposite direction.

3. Stitch two wings as graphed, reverse remaining two wings and work stitches in opposite direction.

4. When background stitching is completed, work black floss Backstitches and Straight Stitches on beaks, tails and leaves, omitting stitch over edge of beak at this time. For eyes, attach sequins to head of bird pieces with black yarn French Knot.

5. Whipstitch wrong sides of leaf pieces together. Matching edges, Whipstitch wing fronts to wing backs.

6. Overcast bottom edges of cardinal pieces between dots. Matching edges, Whipstitch pieces together in beak area with orange, then work black floss stitch over edge for mouth. Whipstitch remaining edges together, stuffing lightly with fiberfill before closing.

7. Glue wings to body as in photo.

Painting

1. Lightly sand tassel top and dowel; wipe clean.

2. Paint dowel light red.

3. Allowing paint to dry between each step, paint head and base on tassel top with dark red; paint midsection with light red, leaving band unpainted. Color band with black permanent marker.

Final Assembly

1. Using photo as a guide throughout assembly, glue red metallic needlepoint yarn around lower edge of band, then tie a length of red metallic needlepoint yarn in a bow and glue to seam.

2. Thread one end of wire through hole in beak where indicated on graph; wrap wire around edge and thread through hole again, leaving a small tail.

3. Repeat instructions in step 2 with remaining end of wire, threading through hole indicated in leaf instead of through beak and leaving a tail. Curl all wire around pencil. Glue pompoms to top part of leaf.

4. Insert one end of dowel through hole in tassel top all the way to the bottom. Turn upside down and drip hot glue inside to secure dowel.

5. Place glue on remaining end of dowel and insert in opening at bottom of bird, leaving about 5 inches of dowel exposed. ●

Skill Level

Intermediate

Size

Approximately 10½ inches W x 17 inches H

Materials

- 1½ sheets 7-count plastic canvas
- Coats & Clark Red Heart Classic worsted weight yarn Art. E267 as listed in color key
- Coats & Clark Red Heart Kids worsted weight yarn Art. E711 as listed in color key
- ⅛-inch-wide Plastic Canvas 7 Metallic Needlepoint Yarn from Rainbow Gallery as listed in color key
- 6-strand embroidery floss as listed in color key
- #16 tapestry needle
- #24 tapestry needle
- Small amount fiberfill
- 12 inches black 24-gauge wire
- 2 (8mm) gold cup sequins
- 2 (¼-inch) red pompoms
- 12 inches ³/₁₆-inch hardwood dowel
- 5-inch-high x 2¼-inch-diameter Create A Tassel large clown head #84927 wooden tassel top from Toner Plastics
- Acrylic craft paints: light red and dark red (to match yarn colors)
- Paintbrushes
- Black permanent marker
- Sandpaper
- Pencil
- Hot-glue gun

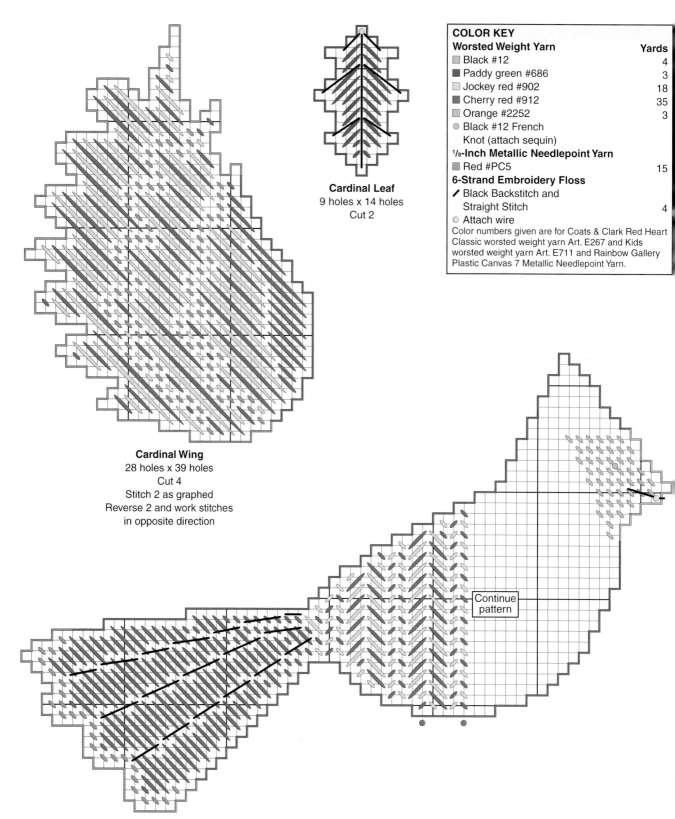

Cardinal Leaf
9 holes x 14 holes
Cut 2

COLOR KEY

Worsted Weight Yarn	Yards
⬜ Black #12	4
⬛ Paddy green #686	3
⬜ Jockey red #902	18
⬛ Cherry red #912	35
⬜ Orange #2252	3
● Black #12 French Knot (attach sequin)	
1/8-Inch Metallic Needlepoint Yarn	
▨ Red #PC5	15
6-Strand Embroidery Floss	
╱ Black Backstitch and Straight Stitch	4
● Attach wire	

Color numbers given are for Coats & Clark Red Heart Classic worsted weight yarn Art. E267 and Kids worsted weight yarn Art. E711 and Rainbow Gallery Plastic Canvas 7 Metallic Needlepoint Yarn.

Cardinal Wing
28 holes x 39 holes
Cut 4
Stitch 2 as graphed
Reverse 2 and work stitches
in opposite direction

Continue
pattern

Cardinal
63 holes x 43 holes
Cut 2
Stitch 1 as graphed
Reverse 1 and work stitches
in opposite direction

Bookworm Reading Glasses Case & Bookmark

This crafty critter turns winter reading into a magic carpet ride full of wonder!

DESIGNS BY JANELLE GIESE

Skill Level
Advanced

Size
Reading Glasses Case: 4 1/8 inches W x 7 inches H, excluding tassels
Bookmark: 2 3/8 inches W x 7 1/2 inches H, excluding tassels

Materials
- 2/3 sheet clear 7-count plastic canvas
- Small amount forest green 7-count plastic canvas
- Small amount clear 10-count plastic canvas
- Uniek Needloft plastic canvas yarn as listed in color key
- Kreinik Heavy (#32) Braid as listed in color key
- Kreinik Medium (#16) Braid as listed in color key
- Kreinik Fine (#8) Braid as listed in color key
- DMC #3 pearl cotton as listed in color key
- DMC #5 pearl cotton as listed in color key
- #16 tapestry needle
- Hot-glue gun

Reading Glasses Case

1. Cut case front and back from clear 7-count plastic canvas according to graphs.

2. Stitch pieces following graphs, working uncoded areas with camel Continental Stitches.

3. When background stitching is completed, use full strands yarn to work eggshell Straight Stitches for pages of book and black Straight Stitches to form pupil of each eye. Use 1 strand eggshell to work Straight Stitches over fern stitches where indicated on bookworm.

4. Use black #3 pearl cotton to embroider features on bookworm and magic carpet. Embroider reading glasses and outline book pages with gold medium braid.

5. For each tassel and hair tuft, bring yarn down through holes indicated, leaving a ¾-inch tail on front. Make a small Straight Stitch through back of stitching, then draw

yarn back up through same hole, again leaving a ¾ inch tail.

6. Using curry heavy braid with tassels and fern yarn with hair tuft, form a tiny Straight Stitch over both ends of yarn in holes indicated to anchor each on front. Trim and fluff tails with a needle.

7. Using forest yarn, Whipstitch wrong sides of case front and back together around side and bottom edges; Overcast top edges.

Bookmark

1. Cut motif from clear 10-count plastic canvas and bookmark from forest green 7-count plastic canvas according to graphs, cutting out three areas indicated on bookmark.

2. Stitch bookmark motif following graph, stopping just above blue highlighted attachment lines. Place motif over bookmark, matching blue lines on motif with blue highlighted area on bookmark, then

work remaining stitches, stitching through both layers. Overcast edges, continuing to join while Overcasting.

3. When background stitching is completed, use off white to work Straight Stitch for pages of book and Straight Stitches over dark pistachio green stitches on bookworm.

4. Work black #5 pearl cotton embroidery, passing over pupil of each eye two times. Embroider reading glasses and outline book pages with gold fine braid.

5. Work tassels and hair tuft with pearl cotton following steps 5 and 6 under reading glasses case, using gold fine braid with tassels and dark pistachio green pearl cotton with hair tuft to anchor each on front. ***Note:*** *Anchor stitch for lowest tassel will be over a bar on bookmark.*

6. Work Running Stitches around perimeter of bookmark with curry heavy braid. ●

COLOR KEY
BOOKMARK

#3 Pearl Cotton	Yards
■ Medium red #304	3
▨ Dark pistachio green #367	1
▨ Very dark violet #550	1
☐ Off white #746	1
■ Very dark garnet #902	1
■ Forest green #989	2
⁄ Off white #746 Straight Stitch	

#5 Pearl Cotton

✎ Black #310 Backstitch and Straight Stitch	1

Heavy (#32) Braid

⁄ Curry #2122 Running Stitch	1

Fine (#8) Braid

⁄ Gold #002 Backstitch and Straight Stitch	1
○ Attach dark pistachio green #367 hair tuft	
● Attach very dark garnet #902 tassels	
♡ Anchor tassel and hair tuft	

Color numbers given are for DMC #3 and #5 pearl cotton and Kreinik Heavy (#32) and Fine (#8) braids.

Bookmark Motif
23 holes x 23 holes
Cut 1 from clear 10-count

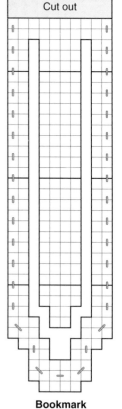

Cut out

Cut out

Bookmark
10 holes x 39 holes
Cut 1 from forest green 7-count

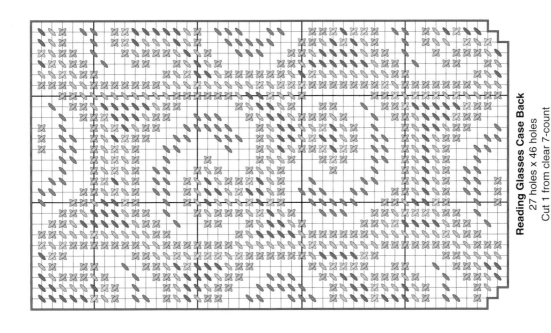

Reading Glasses Case Back
27 holes x 46 holes
Cut 1 from clear 7-count

Reading Glasses Case Front
27 holes x 46 holes
Cut 1 from clear 7-count

COLOR KEY

READING GLASSES CASE

Plastic Canvas Yarn	**Yards**
Black #00	9
Red #01	2
Burgundy #03	6
Fern #23	8
Christmas green #28	1
Forest #29	8
Eggshell #39	1
Purple #46	1
Uncoded areas are camel #43 Continental Stitches	10
Black #00 Straight Stitch
Eggshell #39 Straight Stitch

Heavy (#32) Braid
Curry #2122 | 14

Medium (#16) Braid
Gold #002 Backstitch and Straight Stitch | 1

#3 Pearl Cotton
Black #310 Backstitch and Straight Stitch | 4
● Attach burgundy #03 tassel
● Attach fern #23 hair tuft
● Anchor tassel and hair tuft

Color numbers given are for Uniek Needloft plastic canvas yarn, Kreinik Heavy (#32) and Medium (#16) braids and DMC #3 pearl cotton.

Winter Calendar

Frosty snow friends and perky poinsettias sprinkle the winter months with cheer!

DESIGN BY ANGIE ARICKX

Project Note

Some graphs are shared with similar calendars in other chapters of this book. Colors used for each season are given with the graphs and/or the instructions for that season.

Instructions

1. Following graphs throughout, cut snowmen, poinsettia fronts and poinsettia backs; cut frame front, spacer and fence (pages 24 and 25). Cut one 81-hole x 65-hole piece for calendar frame back.

2. Stitch and Overcast fence with maple. Stitch and Overcast snowmen and poinsettia pieces following graphs, working uncoded areas on snowmen with white Continental Stitches. Work Backstitches and French Knots last.

3. Using holly through step 4, stitch calendar frame front, leaving area shaded with yellow unworked for now. Overcast inside and outside edges.

4. Center spacer, then frame back over unworked area on wrong side of calendar front. **Note:** *Spacer should be between frame front and back.* Complete pattern stitch on frame front in shaded yellow area, working through all three layers.

5. Using photo as a guide throughout, glue poinsettia front to poinsettia backs, spacing fronts so back petals show. Glue fence, snowmen and poinsettias to frame front. Glue hanger to frame back. Insert calendar through opening on right side. ●

Skill Level

Beginner

Size

13¾ inches W x 11 inches H; fits calendar sheet 11 inches W x 8½ inches H

Materials

- 3 sheets 7-count plastic canvas
- Uniek Needloft plastic canvas yarn as listed in color key
- #16 tapestry needle
- Sawtooth hanger
- Hot-glue gun

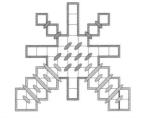

Winter Calendar Poinsettia Back
11 holes x 10 holes
Cut 12

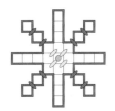

Winter Calendar Poinsettia Front
9 holes x 9 holes
Cut 12

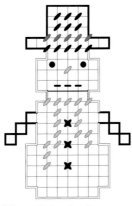

Winter Calendar Snowman
12 holes x 18 holes
Cut 2

COLOR KEY	
Plastic Canvas Yarn	**Yards**
■ Black #00	3
■ Red #01	12
■ Christmas red #02	14
□ Pumpkin #12	1
Maple #13	10
■ Fern #23	12
Holly #27	40
□ Yellow #57	2
Uncoded areas on snowmen are white #41 Continental Stitches	4
⁄ White #41 Overcasting	
⁄ Black #00 Backstitch	
● Black #00 French Knot	
◉ Fern #23 French Knot	
Color numbers given are for Uniek Needloft plastic canvas yarn.	

Winter Bug Welcome

All bundled up and ready for sledding, this bouncy bug greets your guests with a giggle!

DESIGN BY JANELLE GIESE

Skill Level
Advanced

Size
8³⁄₈ inches W x 12¼ inches H

Materials
- 1 sheet stiff 7-count plastic canvas
- Uniek Needloft plastic canvas yarn as listed in color key
- Kreinik Heavy (#32) Braid as listed in color key
- #5 pearl cotton as listed in color key
- #3 pearl cotton as listed in color key
- 1 yard 6-strand embroidery floss to match baby yellow yarn
- #16 tapestry needle
- Sawtooth hanger
- 6 (7mm) nickel jump rings
- Needle-nose pliers

Project Notes
The triangle, heart, star, square, inverted triangle and diamond shapes designate Continental Stitches.

The sign graph is shared with the other bug welcome designs in other chapters of this book. Colors used for each season are given with the graphs and/or the instructions for that season.

Instructions
1. Cut bug (page 162) and sign (page 34) from plastic canvas according to graphs.

2. Stitch and Overcast welcome sign following graph, working uncoded background with eggshell Continental Stitches; replace lavender yarn with lilac yarn.

3. When background stitching on sign is completed, work lilac heavy braid Straight Stitches over lilac yarn Continental Stitches. Using black #3 pearl cotton, embroider remaining portions of lettering.

4. Stitch and Overcast bug, working uncoded areas on face and body with baby yellow Continental Stitches.

5. When background stitching is completed, embroider lilac braid accents on wings. Use a full strand white yarn to Straight Stitch antennae highlights. Work all pearl cotton embroidery

6. Sew sawtooth hanger to top center back of bug's head with 6-strand embroidery floss.

7. Using needle-nose pliers, join bug to sign by forming two chains of three jump rings each, attaching top and bottom jump rings through holes indicated with yellow dots. ●

WELCOME

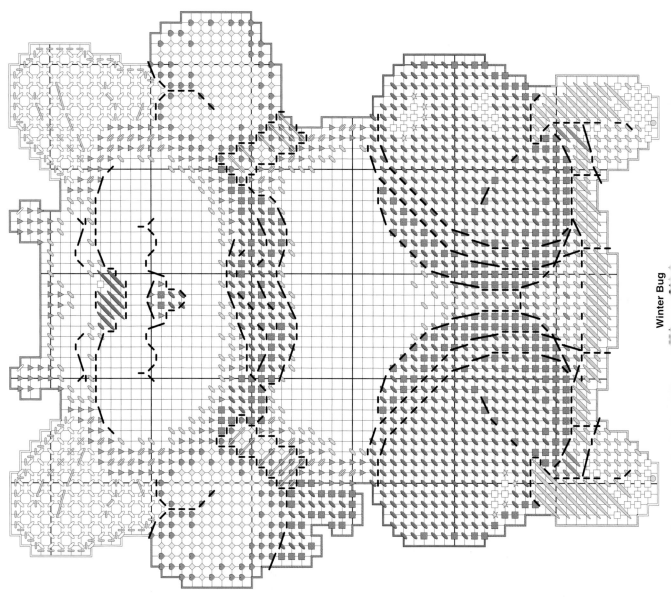

Winter Bug

COLOR KEY

	Plastic Canvas Yarn	**Yards**
▽	Black #00	7
◤	Red #01	11
■	Burgundy #03	6
☆	Silver #37	1
◢	Gray #38	3
◎	Eggshell #39	11
◢	Beige #40	7
□	White #41	2
◢	Camel #43	2
◈	Lilac #45	2
●	Turquoise #54	4
△	Bright blue #60	3
	Uncoded backgrounds on bug face and body are baby yellow #21 Continental Stitches	10
	Uncoded background on welcome sign is eggshell #39 Continental Stitches	
◎	White #41 Straight Stitch	
	Heavy (#32) Braid	
◢	Lilac #023 Backstitch and Straight Stitch	3
	#3 Pearl Cotton	
◢	Black Backstitch and Straight Stitch	10
	#5 Pearl Cotton	
◢	Black Backstitch and Straight Stitch	1

Color numbers given are for Uniek Needloft plastic canvas yarn and Kreinik Heavy (#32) Braid.

Santa's Bee Merry Garland

With his new sleigh team leading the way, Santa is all "abuzz" about spreading joy this season!

DESIGN BY JUDY COLLISHAW

Cutting & Stitching

1. Cut plastic canvas according to graphs (pages 164 and 165).

2. Stitch and Overcast sleigh and arm following graphs, working uncoded areas with red Continental Stitches.

3. Stitch and Overcast flag, working uncoded background on flag with white Continental Stitches; Backstitch and Overcast flag pole with dark red copper.

Skill Level

Beginner

Size

36 inches W x 7¼ inches H

Materials

- 1 sheet 7-count plastic canvas
- Worsted weight yarn as listed in color key
- #5 pearl cotton as listed in color key
- #16 tapestry needle
- 41 inches ¼-inch-wide green satin ribbon
- 3 (12mm) gold jingle bells
- 2 (¼-inch) black pompoms
- ¼-inch red pompom
- 5mm red pompom
- Hand-sewing needle
- Green sewing thread to match ribbon
- Hot-glue gun

4. Stitch and Overcast bee bodies, heads and wings, Overcasting nose edges on one bee head with red as graphed; Overcast nose edges on remaining two heads with black.

5. When background stitching is completed, use a full strand yarn to work Straight Stitches for Santa's mustache; work French Knots for eyes on Santa and bees, wrapping yarn one time around needle. Use 2-ply black yarn to work doll's French Knot eyes, wrapping needle one time.

6. Using red floss, Backstitch lettering on flag and mouth on doll.

Assembly

1. Using photo as a guide throughout assembly, glue ¼-inch red pompom to nose of bee with red Overcasting. Glue black pompoms to noses of remaining two bees. Glue 5mm pompom to center of Santa's face for nose.

2. Glue heads to front of bee bodies; glue wings in pairs to tops of bees. Glue flag pole behind Santa's raised hand and tip of flag to tip of Santa's hat.

3. Cut two 10-inch lengths of green ribbon. Glue ends of each length together to form two separate loops. Glue ends of one loop behind head of red-nosed bee; glue ends of remaining loop behind arm of doll on sleigh.

4. Glue left end of remaining 21-inch length of ribbon to wrong side of red-nosed bee along top edge. Glue remaining bees to ribbon, allowing 6 inches between bees.

5. Glue right end of ribbon behind hand on Santa's arm, then glue arm to front of Santa's body.

6. Using hand-sewing needle and green sewing thread, center and attach jingle bells to ribbon between bees and to ribbon immediately in front of sleigh. ●

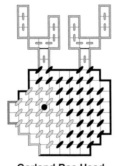

Garland Bee Wing
7 holes x 11 holes
Cut 6

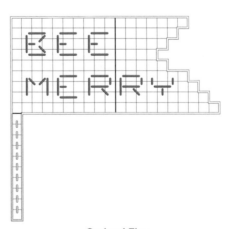

Garland Bee Body
26 holes x 15 holes
Cut 3

Garland Bee Head
10 holes x 14 holes
Cut 3
Overcast 1 as graphed
Overcast nose area on 2
replacing red with black

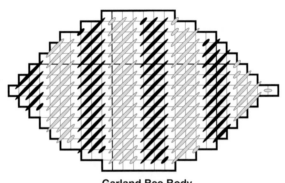

Garland Flag
20 holes x 19 holes
Cut 1

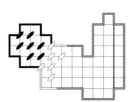

Garland Santa Arm
11 holes x 8 holes
Cut 1

COLOR KEY

Worsted Weight Yarn	Yards
■ Black	12
☐ White	11
☐ Deep yellow	8
■ Kelly green	5
☐ Dark beige brown	3
☐ Gray	3
■ Dark brown	1
☐ Cream	1
☐ Pale yellow	1
☐ Medium blue	1
■ Burgundy	1
☐ Pale peach	1
☐ Rose	1
Uncoded background on flag is white Continental Stitches	
Uncoded areas on Santa's sleigh and arm are red Continental Stitches	5
⁄ Red Overcasting	
⁄ Dark red copper Backstitch and Overcasting	1
⁄ Gray Backstitch	
⁄ Dark beige brown	
⁄ Cream Straight Stitch	
● Black (4-ply) French Knot	
● Black (2-ply) French Knot	
6-Strand Embroidery Floss	
⁄ Red Backstitch	1

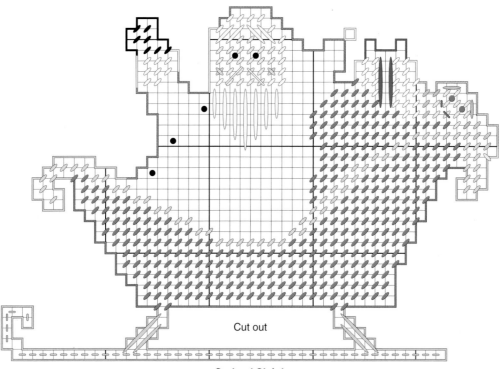

Cut out

Garland Sleigh
48 holes x 33 holes
Cut 1

Gingerbug

Frosted with friendliness, this "bug on the wall" calls a gingerbread house a home!

DESIGN BY LAURA P. VICTORY

Skill Level
Beginner

Size
9¼ inches W x 9½ inches H

Materials
- 5-inch Uniek QuickShape plastic canvas hexagon
- 3-inch plastic canvas radial circle
- Uniek Needloft plastic canvas yarn as listed in color key
- #16 tapestry needle
- 28 inches ½-inch-wide white iridescent medium rickrack #427-001 from Wrights
- 2 (15mm) movable eyes
- Red gum drop button
- 4 (⅝-inch) round green peppermint buttons
- 2 candy cane buttons
- 1 heart-shaped peppermint button or 2 candy cane buttons
- 6 (12-inch) red glitter chenille stems
- 2 (½-inch) red glitter pompoms
- Glitter
- White glue
- Hot-glue gun

COLOR KEY

Plastic Canvas Yarn	Yards
☐ Maple #13	21
⁄ Red #01 and white	
#41 Backstitch	1 each
⁄ Maple #13 Straight Stitch	

Color numbers given are for Uniek Needloft plastic canvas yarn.

Instructions

1. Stitch and Overcast pieces following graphs, working stitches from center out in each section of hexagon.

2. When background stitching is completed, work maple Straight Stitches on body. Combine red and white yarn; knot end. Twist together, then Backstitch mouth for a peppermint candy look.

3. Using photo as guide and hot glue through step 6, glue rickrack to front of head around edge and to body just inside Straight Stitches along edges.

4. For antennae, glue two candy cane buttons to top of head, then glue red pompoms to tops of candy canes.

5. Glue red gum drop button in center of circle for nose and movable eyes above nose. Glue heart-shaped button or two candy cane buttons arranged in a heart shape to center of body for belly button. Glue green peppermint buttons around belly button.

6. Glue head to top of body. Bend red chenille stems in half and glue to back-side of body for legs.

7. Apply a light coat of white glue to cheeks on head and to body, keeping eyes free of glue. Sprinkle with glitter while still wet. Allow to dry.

8. Hang as desired. ●

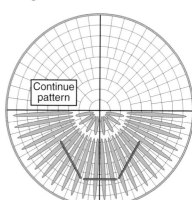

Gingerbug Head
Stitch 1

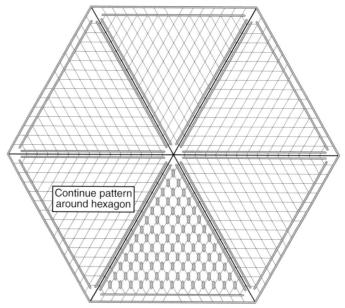

Gingerbug Body
Stitch 1

Peppermint Bug

Indulge your sweet tooth with this clever candy critter!

DESIGN BY LAURA P. VICTORY

Skill Level
Beginner

Size
8³⁄₈ inches W x 9 inches H

Materials
- ¼ sheet 7-count plastic canvas
- 3-inch plastic canvas radial circle
- Uniek Needloft plastic canvas yarn as listed in color key
- 6-strand embroidery floss as listed in color key
- #16 tapestry needle
- 2 (15mm) movable eyes
- 3 (½-inch) gold jingle bells
- Green gum drop button
- 3 (⁵⁄₈-inch) round green peppermint buttons
- 5 (6-inch) green glitter chenille stems
- Pencil
- 4 (½-inch) red glitter pompoms
- Glitter
- White glue
- Hot-glue gun

COLOR KEY

Plastic Canvas Yarn	Yards
■ Red #02	3
□ White #41	16
Uncoded areas on front are white #41 Continental Stitches	
╱ Red #02 Backstitch	
6-Strand Embroidery Floss	
╱ Red Backstitch	5
● Attach leg	
Color numbers given are for Uniek Needloft plastic canvas yarn.	

Instructions

1. Cut body from 7-count plastic canvas according to graphs. Do not cut plastic canvas radial circle, which will be the head.

2. Stitch and Overcast pieces following graphs, working uncoded areas on body with white Continental Stitches.

3. When background stitching is completed, work red yarn Backstitches for mouth and red embroidery floss Backstitches, outlining red stripes on body.

4. Using photo as a guide through step 7, for legs, thread one jingle bell on each of three green chenille stems to midpoint, then fold in half, and twist once about ½-inch from fold. Thread ends from front to back through holes indicated on graph, twist ends of each leg together then tack in place with yarn on backside.

5. For antennae, wrap remaining two lengths of green chenille stems around pencil to coil. Hot glue to back of head, then glue one red pompom to top of each antenna.

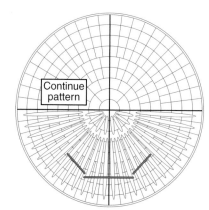

Peppermint Bug Head
Stitch 1

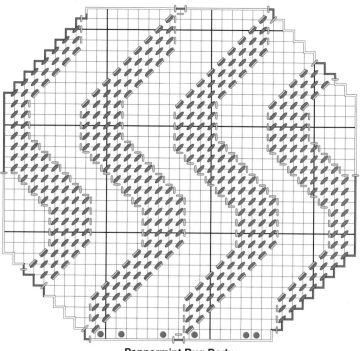

Peppermint Bug Body
34 holes x 32 holes
Cut 1

6. Using hot glue throughout, glue as follows: green gum drop button in center of circle for nose, movable eyes above nose and remaining two red pompoms to head for cheeks.

7. Apply a light coat of white glue to white strips on body, around edges of head and to head around nose, eyes, cheeks and mouth, keeping facial features free of glue. Sprinkle with glitter while still wet. Allow to dry.

8. Hot glue head to top left corner of body, then center and glue round green peppermint buttons to body front.

9. Hang as desired. ●

Goose Doorstop

Let your friends "take a gander" at this garland-bearing goose!

DESIGN BY KATHLEEN HURLEY

Skill Level
Beginner

Size
11 inches W x 7⅞ inches H x
3 inches D

Materials
- 3 sheets 7-count plastic canvas
- Uniek Needloft plastic canvas yarn as listed in color key
- #16 tapestry needle
- Brick

Instructions

1. Cut plastic canvas according to graphs (pages 171 and 172). Doorstop base will remain unstitched.

2. Stitch and Overcast goose and wing following graphs, working uncoded areas on wing with gray Continental Stitches.

3. When background stitching is completed, work gray Backstitches and red French Knots, then work white Turkey Loop Stitches on hat cuff and hat tip (shaded blue areas), making loops about ⅜ inch long. Cut loops and trim as needed.

4. Stitch doorstop front, back, ends and top following graphs.

5. Using red throughout, Whipstitch front and back to ends, then Whipstitch front, back and ends to top.

6. Using photo as a guide throughout, tack wing to goose at wing front between arrows and at wing tip using white yarn. Tack goose to doorstop front with a few hidden stitches, making sure bottom edges are even.

7. Using red, Whipstitch base to assembled doorstop, inserting brick before closing. ●

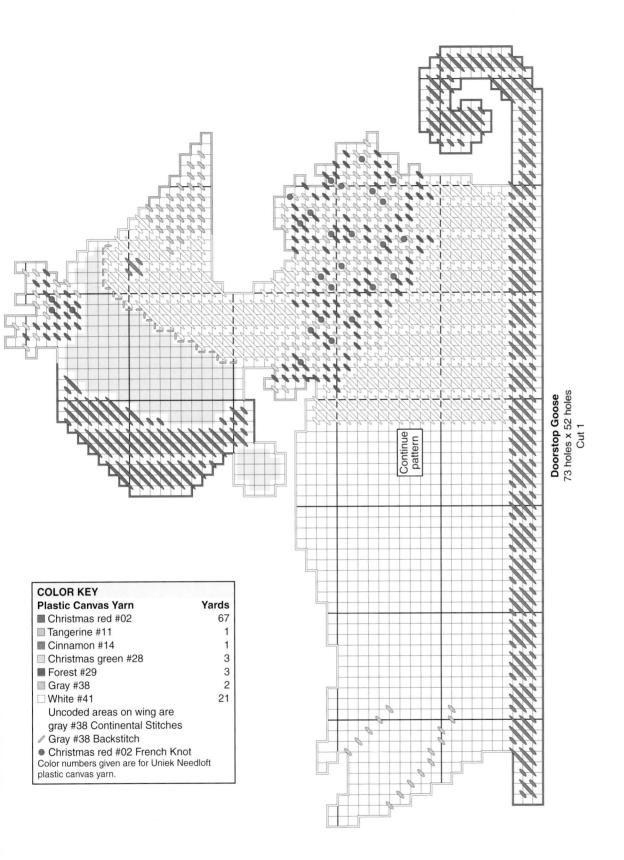

Doorstop Goose
73 holes x 52 holes
Cut 1

Continue pattern

COLOR KEY

Plastic Canvas Yarn	Yards
■ Christmas red #02	67
▨ Tangerine #11	1
▨ Cinnamon #14	1
▨ Christmas green #28	3
■ Forest #29	3
▨ Gray #38	2
□ White #41	21

Uncoded areas on wing are
gray #38 Continental Stitches
╱ Gray #38 Backstitch
● Christmas red #02 French Knot
Color numbers given are for Uniek Needloft
plastic canvas yarn.

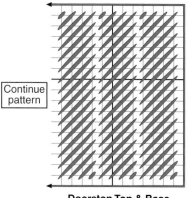

Doorstop Top & Base
57 holes x 17 holes
Cut 2, stitch 1

Continue pattern

COLOR KEY

Plastic Canvas Yarn	Yards
■ Christmas red #02	67
☐ Tangerine #11	1
■ Cinnamon #14	1
☐ Christmas green #28	3
■ Forest #29	3
■ Gray #38	2
☐ White #41	21
Uncoded areas on wing are gray #38 Continental Stitches	
⁄ Gray #38 Backstitch	
● Christmas red #02 French Knot	

Color numbers given are for Uniek Needloft plastic canvas yarn.

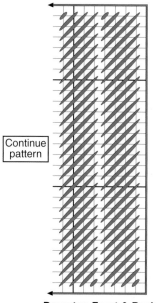

Continue pattern

Doorstop Front & Back
57 holes x 27 holes
Cut 2

Doorstop End
17 holes x 27 holes
Cut 2

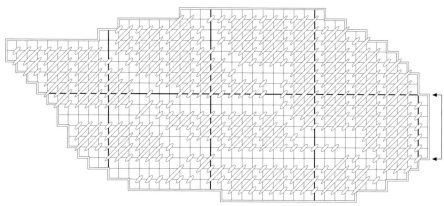

Doorstop Goose Wing
41 holes x 18 holes
Cut 1

Special Thanks

We would like to acknowledge and thank the following designers whose original work has been published in this collection. We appreciate and value their creativity and dedication to designing quality plastic canvas projects!

Angie Arickx
Autumn Birdhouse Hideaway, Autumn Calendar, Purple Rose Vanity Tray, Spring Calendar, Summer Calendar, Winter Calendar

Janna Britton
Bee Happy, Bug Fun Bookmarks, Flutterbugs Puppets, Happy Frog Tote, Ladybug Dreams Journal

Ronda Bryce
Flower Basket Wall Hanging

Pam Bull
Autumn Bugs, Winter Dragonfly

Judy Collishaw
Bumbly Bee Napkin Ring, Santa's Bee Merry Garland

Mary T. Cosgrove
Mallard Frame, Spring Posy Pin, Vase of Bittersweet

Janelle Giese
Autumn Bug Welcome, Bookworm Reading Glasses Case & Bookmark, Flower Vendor Centerpiece, Luminescent Candlesticks, Mother's Nest, Mystic Butterfly Candle Platform, Spring Bug Welcome, Summer Bug Welcome, Sunflower Garden Coasters, Vintage Rose Tissue Topper, Winter Bug Welcome, Winter Floral Match Box

Robin Howard Will
Island Paradise

Kathleen Hurley
Flights of Fancy, Goose Doorstop, Partridge in a Pear Tree Wreath

Susan Leinberger
Blossoms & Bluebirds, Centipede Memo Magnets, Country Crow, Critter Catcher Kit, Cute As a Bug Dresser Set, Honey-Do List

Lee Lindeman
Chubby Baby Birdies, Pot of Daffodils

Kristine Loffredo
Springtime Violets Coaster Set

Alida Macor
A Touch of Autumn, Tulip Picnic Pockets, Midnight Violets Eyeglasses Case

Joyce Messenger
Poinsettia Tissue Topper

Sue Penrod
Butterfly Bookmark, Ladybug Photo Album, Wineglass Rings

Robin Petrina
Dragonfly Box, Dragonfly Pin

Terry Ricioli
Cardinal, Chickadee

Ruby Thacker
Butterflies & Blooms Tic-Tac-Toe, Friends in Flight

Laura P. Victory
Gingerbug, Night Light Bug, Peppermint Bug

Kathy Wirth
Blossom Doily & Napkin Ring, Cardinal on a Stick , Dancing Daffodils Tissue Topper, Pansy Coasters & Holder, Robin on a Stick

Buyer's Guide
When looking for a specific material, first check your local craft and retail stores. If you are unable to locate a product locally, contact the manufacturers listed below for the closest retail source in your area or a mail-order source.

The Beadery
P.O. Box 178
Hope Valley, RI 02832
(401) 539-2432
www.thebeadery.com

Blumenthal Lansing Co.
1929 Main St.
Lansing, IA 52151
(563) 538-4211
www.buttonsplus.com

**C.M. Offray & Son Inc./
Lion Ribbon Co. Inc.**
Rte. 24, Box 601
Chester, NJ 07930
(800) 551-LION
www.offray.com

Coats & Clark Inc.
Consumer Service
P.O. Box 12229
Greenville, SC 29612-0229
(800) 648-1479
www.coatsandclark.com

Darice
Mail-order source:
Schrock's International
P.O. Box 538
Bolivar, OH 44612
(330) 874-3700

DMC Corp.
Hackensack Ave., Bldg. 10A
South Kearny, NJ 07032-4688
(800) 275-4117
www.dmc-usa.com

Elmore-Pisgah Inc.
204 Oak St.
Spindale, NC 28160
(800) 633-7829
www.elmore-pisgah.com

Gay Bowles Sales Inc.
P.O. Box 1060
Janesville, WI 53547
(800) 447-1332
www.millhill.com

Kreinik Mfg. Co. Inc.
3106 Lord Baltimore Dr. #101
Baltimore, MD 21244-2871
(800) 537-2166
www.kreinik.com

Plaid Enterprises Inc.
3225 Westech Dr.
Norcross, Ga 30092
(800) 842-4197
www.plaidonline.com

Rainbow Gallery
7412 Fulton Ave., #5
North Hollywood, CA 91605
(818)982-4496
www.rainbowgallery.com

Toner Plastics
699 Silver St.
Agawam, MA 01001
(413) 789-1300
www.tonerplastics.com

Uniek
Mail-order source:
Annie's Attic
1 Annie Ln.
Big Sandy, TX 75755
(800) 582-6643
www.anniesattic.com

Wrights
P.O. Box 398
West Warren, MA 01092
(877) 597-4448
www.wrights.com

Yarn Tree Designs Inc.
P.O. Box 724
Ames, IA 50010
(800) 247-3952
www.yarntree.com

Stitch Guide

Use the following diagrams to expand your plastic canvas stitching skills. For each diagram, bring needle up through canvas at the red number one and go back down through the canvas at the red number two. The second stitch is numbered in green. Always bring needle up through the canvas at odd numbers and take it back down through the canvas at the even numbers.

Background Stitches

The following stitches are used for filling in large areas of canvas. The Continental Stitch is the most commonly used stitch. Other stitches, such as the Condensed Mosaic and Scotch Stitch, fill in large areas of canvas more quickly than the Continental Stitch because their stitches cover a larger area of canvas.

Continental Stitch

Condensed Mosaic

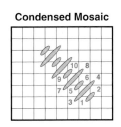

Alternating Continental

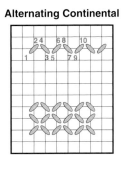

Cross Stitch

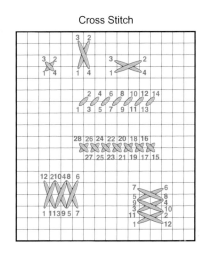

Long Stitch

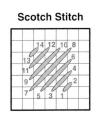

Scotch Stitch

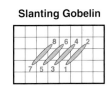

Slanting Gobelin

Embroidery Stitches

These stitches are worked on top of a stitched area to add detail to the project. Embroidery stitches are usually worked with one strand of yarn, several strands of pearl cotton or several strands of embroidery floss.

Lattice Stitch

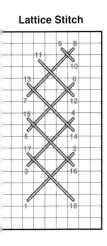

Chain Stitch

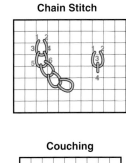

Straight Stitch

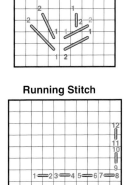

Fly Stitch

Couching

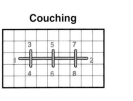

Running Stitch

Backstitch

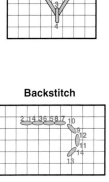

Embroidery Stitches

French Knot

Bring needle up through canvas. Wrap yarn around needle 1 to 3 times, depending on desired size of knot; take needle back through canvas through same hole.

Lazy Daisy

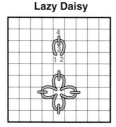

Bring yarn needle up through canvas, then back down in same hole, leaving a small loop.
Then, bring needle up inside loop; take needle back down through canvas on other side of loop.

Loop Stitch/Turkey Loop Stitch

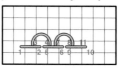

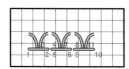

The top diagram shows this stitch left intact. This is an effective stitch for giving a project dimensional hair. The bottom diagram demonstrates the cut loop stitch. Because each stitch is anchored, cutting it will not cause the stitches to come out. A group of cut loop stitches gives a fluffy, soft look and feel to your project.

Specialty Stitches

The following stitches can be worked either on top of a previously stitched area or directly onto the canvas. Like the embroidery stitches, these too add wonderful detail and give your stitching additional interest and texture.

Satin Stitches

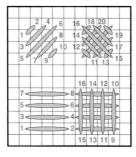

Smyrna Cross

Finishing Stitches

Overcast/Whipstitch

Overcasting and Whipstitching are used to finish the outer edges of the canvas. Overcasting is done to finish one edge at a time. Whipstitching is used to stitch two or more pieces of canvas together along an edge. For both Overcasting and Whipstitching, work one stitch in each hole along straight edges and inside corners, and two or three stitches in outside corners.

Lark's Head Knot

The Lark's Head Knot is used for a fringe edge or for attaching a hanging loop.